The Analyzed Bible

The Analyzed Bible

John

G. Campbell Morgan

BAKER BOOK HOUSE

Grand Rapids, Michigan 49506

First published 1909 by
Hodder and Stoughton
Paperback edition issued 1984 by
Baker Book House

ISBN: 0-8010-6173-3

Printed in the United States of America

CONTENTS

Contents

GOD MANIFEST (*continued*)

Contents

PREFACE

JOHN was a mystic in all the highest senses of the word. Conscious at once of the things patent, and of that vast realm of the spiritual, of which the material is but a partial and transitory manifestation, he came into fellowship with the profoundest things in the Person of his Lord. Turning to the gospel according to John, we find ourselves immediately compelled to worship. The same personality is presented to us as that with which we have grown familiar in the earlier stories. From the beginning, however, we are conscious of a new assertion on the part of the writer, and a new quality about the Person. As we proceed, we find that the change is not that of difference, but an unveiling and explanation. The revelation of this gospel is that of God manifest in flesh. The central division dealing with this is introduced by a brief but pregnant one, showing how the Word came from the everlasting conditions into those of time and human sense; and is followed by one presenting Him in the new everlasting conditions arising out of His incarnate presence in human history. These divisions therefore may thus be stated: From Everlasting (i. 1-18); God Manifest (i. 19-xix.); To Everlasting (xx., xxi.).

John

A. FROM EVERLASTING. I. 1-18

JOHN

A. FROM EVERLASTING

THIS first division of the Gospel of John is intensive rather than extensive. It constitutes a prelude to all that is to follow, introducing us to the subject, and indicating the scope.

The matter of supreme importance in studying it, is that the mind should be kept steadily upon the one Person referred to throughout. That Person is seen in different relationships, but the identity does not change. "The Word," "the Only begotten from the Father," "Jesus Christ," "the Only begotten Son," are different descriptions of one Person. To this Person the perpetually recurring pronouns refer. The whole division sets this Person before us in His cosmic relationships. He is seen in His relation to God; in His relation to the whole creation; in His relation to the processes of redemption; in His relation to individual souls. Our analysis shows the order of the statement.

We are first introduced to the Word essentially; that is to say, He is set before us as to what He is in Himself, and in His relation to that order in the midst of which human life is lived. Finally, in one brief but all-inclusive declaration, the Word is presented to us evangelically; that is, the supreme value of the incarnation is set forth in a simple and yet sublime statement. Between these principal sections, the voices of two witnesses are heard; the first, that of the last representative of the preliminary economy, which culminated in the Christ; the second, that of an apostle of the new, which proceeds from the Christ.

I. THE WORD ESSENTIALLY

In this section the Person is presented to us in two essential relationships which

4

include the whole fact of His Being ; and in relation to the two creations, of both of which He is the Source and Agent.

i. THE TWO RELATIONS

We are immediately introduced to the full glory of this mysterious Person. Nothing so easily blinds as light, and here the light is so intense that it can only be appreciated as it is seen through that second declaration of the temporal manifestation. The three-fold statement concerning the age-abiding facts is one which gathers into itself truths already accepted by the older economy. Throughout the ancient Hebrew writings there is evident recognition of all that is here declared. Explanation or formal statement there had never been, but, under different forms of expression, such as " the Word of God," " Wisdom," " the Angel of His Presence," there had been recognition of a fact not fully comprehended. The second declaration is that which was new and startling, namely, " the Word became flesh." Herein is seen the great value of that historic fact, which this Gospel describes, in its relation to abiding truth. The ideas of the past, never perfectly understood, were now unveiled and brought within the sphere of human observation and comprehension. The same mystic truth personified by such phrases as have been quoted, now appeared centralised in a human Being.

Placing over against each other the comprehensive statement of the first verse and that of the fourteenth, it is seen how they answer each other perfectly.

The first is threefold.

1. Concerning the fact of His existence. " In the beginning was the Word." This is a glimpse of a fact preceding the beginnings of created things.

2. Concerning the law or order of His existence. "The Word was with God." The word "with" here means more than being in the company of. It suggests interaction and communion.

3. Concerning the nature of His being. "The Word was God." This is a simple and sublime statement, leaving no room for misapprehension.

The second is threefold also. This may best be shown by tabulation of these in relation to the first three.

1. "In the beginning was the Word."

1. "Full of grace and truth."

2. "The Word was with God."

2. "Dwelt among us."

3. "The Word was God."

3. "The Word became flesh."

ii. THE TWO CREATIONS

The relation of the Word to the first creation is declared to be that of life and light. Still remembering the nature of the Person as declared in the first verse, we are now told that He was with God in actual co-operation in the creation of all things ; and moreover, that no developments in creation, succeeding the first movement, have been without Him. In one brief sentence, " In Him was life," we are taught that every form of life is derived from Him. It is of the utmost importance that the value of this declaration should not be minimised. The distinction between the life of man, and all lower forms thereof, is recognised in the statement that " the life was the light of men." In man life is more than sensient, in the lower sense in which that word may be used of that which comes next to him in the scale of being; it is intelligent, in the sense of ability to recognise and inquire concerning causes and effects. Perhaps the old distinction between instinct and reason may be allowed to illustrate the difference. In this declaration then, it is taught that this light is directly due to the will and power of this same Person. A further statement of the relation of the Word to the first creation is, that this light has shined through all the darkness, and upon it darkness has never been able to lay arrest. Conscience and the consciousness of right, which are the ultimate values of this light in human life, have always been the result of His shining.

The relation of the Word to the second creation is introduced by reference to John, who was the herald of the advent of the Word. His mission was that of bearing witness to the light; that is, to this light which had always shined, and which darkness had never been able to put out. He came, not the light, but that he might bear witness to it. His ministry was that of calling men to walk in a light which they already had, and that of declaring to them that it was about to shine in a new way, and with new glory. Having made this declaration, the writer, his eye evidently fixed upon the Person of Jesus, breaks out into the affirmation, " There was the true Light . . . coming into the world." This light, which had been in all human life, was now seen coming into clear shining in the Person of One Who in flesh dwelt among men. It was not a new presence, but a new manifestation. A gracious suggestion of love is made in the declaration that He came. He Who was the Origin of created things, came into the midst of His own

9

things, but the people who were His own
"received Him not." Then immediately
the mystery and marvel of the new creation
is referred to. Out of rejection comes a
new reception. All the process is not here
declared, but the fact is announced, of a new
mystery of life springing out of the midst
of the darkness created by the rejection
of the light. Those receiving Him, receive
from Him authority to become children of
God. This authority is that of the new life
received directly from God through Him.

II. THE WITNESSES

To the truth of all that has been declared concerning this Person, a double
witness is then recorded. The first is that
of John, the last of the illustrious line of
Hebrew prophets, who declared that in
the Person of Jesus there was fulfilment
of all that he had foretold. The second
is that of John the apostle, who wrote
out of the actual experience of himself,
and of others, of the reception of the
fulness of the Word.

III. THE WORD EVANGELICALLY

The third section compressed into one brief statement, is the declaration of all that is to be unfolded in the subsequent teaching of the book. Human need is declared in the statement, " No man hath seen God at any time," and Divine provision is announced in the declaration, " The only begotten Son, Which is in the bosom of the Father, He hath declared Him."

Thus the first division of the Gospel shows that the coming of Jesus was that of a Divine movement toward man. The essential and abiding facts conditioning human life were wrought out into visibility in order to the saving of men. Light was focussed in a Person. Life was manifest in a Man. Love operated in the veiled unveiling of human existence. Upon all the things of the earth, and especially upon human life, the light of God's life and love falls in a new and radiant revelation.

11

B. GOD MANIFEST

From this point attention is centred upon the historic Person of Jesus as the One through Whom God is manifest in time. The selection of words and works is so far chronological as to indicate a threefold movement in this manifestation. Matters of the more public ministry of Jesus are first recorded, which show how God was manifest in the world. Then follows a careful account of those final and private discourses to His disciples, which reveal how God is manifest to His own. Finally the last things of His suffering, dying, and resurrection are told, so as to show how God is manifest by the Cross.

I. IN THE WORLD

The section dealing with the manifestation in the world consists of a Prologue, introducing the herald and the first disciples ; the main system setting forth the essential revelation ; and an Epilogue, giving illustrations of results following.

i. THE PROLOGUE

a. THE HERALD

This section is an elaboration of the declaration made in the first division of the book. "John beareth witness of Him, and crieth, saying, This was He of Whom I said, He that cometh after me is become before me: for He was before me." The testimony is emphatic in the distinction it draws between John Baptist and Jesus, as the prophet himself understood that distinction. It consists of replies to inquiries, and formal proclamations.

A deputation had been sent to John consisting of priests and Levites, charged to inquire concerning himself and his work. This gave him the opportunity of making perfectly clear that the nature of his mission was relative rather than personal. The first enquiry of the deputation related to himself. His ministry had been a most remarkable one in the interest and enthusiasm which it had evoked. It was impossible for the rulers to ignore it, and

14

they now desired a definite declaration from him as to his claims. They demanded simply to know who he was in the words, " Who art thou ? " To this he immediately replied, " I am not the Christ," thus answering in all probability a suspicion which they entertained as to the claim he would make, and at the same time preparing the way for that declaration of the imminent advent of Messiah which was the final burden of his ministry.

They next asked him, " Art thou Elijah ? " and their question was the outcome of a popular conception, that before the coming of the Deliverer, the ancient prophet would himself reappear. This materialistic idea he immediately corrected by answering, " I am not." Finally they asked him if he were " the prophet," reference undoubtedly being made to the promise of Moses (Deut. xviii. 15), and he replied in the briefest of negatives.

So far he had not satisfied them, and again they asked him, " What sayest thou of thyself ? " To that inquiry he replied by a quotation from their own prophet Isaiah, the full significance of which can only be discovered by noticing the place of the quotation in the book of Isaiah. Such observation will show that the claim of John was one which was calculated to arouse in his hearers the spirit of expectation, and to turn attention from himself to the coming One. He was standing in the light of the advent of the Messiah, and his own person and mission were seen to be of little importance save as they heralded Another. He was "the voice," the Word was approaching.

Their next inquiry related to his work. The interest of the Pharisees naturally centred upon the ritual of baptism, and they demanded the meaning of his baptism, seeing that he was neither the Christ, nor Elijah, nor the prophet. Thus again they gave him the opportunity of directing their attention from himself to the coming One. His baptism was " in water," a thing purely material and symbolic. One, already in the midst of them, had standing of such

dignity that John did not feel himself
worthy even to be His slave. Yet this
One they had not discovered. He was unknown, for He " hath no form nor comeliness " that they " should desire Him."

The day following the visit of the
deputation the prophet made his public
proclamation concerning Jesus. It is important to notice the relation of this
proclamation to things not chronicled by
John. It is perfectly certain that it was
made after His baptism, for immediately
following it Jesus turned to His public
ministry, and was followed by some disciples of John. It is equally patent therefore that it was subsequent to the temptation. In this Gospel only those crises in
the life of the Lord which are more
closely related to His Deity are recorded.
These are the Incarnation, the Crucifixion,
and the Resurrection. The four which are
more intimately associated with His human
nature are omitted. These are the Baptism,
the Temptation, the Transfiguration, and
the Ascension.

Remembering the order of the life of
Jesus as revealed in the other three
Gospels, it becomes evident that after His
baptism, in which John saw the Spirit
descend upon Him, Jesus had passed into
the wilderness to temptation. Returning
therefrom, and ere setting His face to
the exercise of His public ministry, He
revisited John. This approach occurred
on the day after the deputation had been
sent to the prophet. Beholding Him,
John, in carefully chosen words, proclaimed
Him, and announced with equal care the
method by which he identified Him. A
study of the paragraph containing this
proclamation shows the process in the mind
and ministry of John. In his commission
to preach and baptize, a commission received in the loneliness of the wilderness,
it had been distinctly communicated to
him that in the course of his work One
would appear to him, upon Whom he
would see the Spirit descending and abiding.
By that sign he was to know the One
Whose mission would be that of passing

from the material to the spiritual, substituting the baptism of the Spirit for that of water.

That vision had been granted to John when he baptized Jesus of Nazareth. Now he proclaimed Him in words which must be interpreted by his relation to the Hebrew economy. As he had himself claimed to be the voice predicted by Isaiah, he now identified Jesus as " the Lamb of God," also fully described by Isaiah in prophecies following upon those in which his own mission had been foretold. Not only did he thus identify Him, but in clearest language declared the deepest meaning of His mission in the words, "that taketh away the sin of the world." His final statement shows that he recognised not only the official position of Jesus, but also His essential nature. " I have seen, and have borne witness."

Once again, on the next day the eyes of John rested upon Jesus. The expression "he looked upon" suggests a penetrating glance. The word only occurs once again

19

in the Gospel, where it is said that Jesus looked upon Simon. It was a look of perfect comprehension. At the moment, Jesus was walking away, His face set toward His own ministry, with all that it involved of teaching and doing and suffering. The whole meaning for John found fullest expression in the simple declaration, "Behold the Lamb of God." Thus again, and finally, he turned the attention of those who had gathered to his ministry from himself to the Word, and in so doing fulfilled his mission.

The supreme value of this section is indicated in the opening words, "This is the witness of John." While with perfect naturalness the story is told in such a way as to show the method by which John bore his witness, it is of supreme importance that the testimony itself be detached from all the merely local setting. If this be done it will become evident that this last and greatest of the Hebrew prophets had been supremely impressed with the teaching of his illustrious pre-

decessor, Isaiah. Every declaration concerning Jesus was an allusion to some
statement contained in the book of Isaiah,
and the whole proclamation reveals his
sense of the fulfilment of Isaiah's vision in
the Person of Jesus.

When he spoke of himself as "the
voice" fulfilling the foretelling of Isaiah,
his meaning can only be interpreted by
an examination of that prediction. It
occurs in the fortieth chapter of the
prophecy, and there reference to the voice
is but incidental. The message delivered
was one which indicated the advent of
Jehovah to move along a highway flung
up in the wilderness for the redemption
of His people. If John were that voice,
the One Whose coming he heralded, was
Jehovah.

Following Isaiah's prophecy, we presently
see the One foretold passing along a pathway of suffering, and the prophet breaks out
into the lament of the fifty-third chapter,
over the fact that in the midst of His
people He was unrecognised and unappre-

ciated, "a root out of a dry ground: He hath no form nor comeliness; and when we see Him, there is no beauty that we should desire Him." All this was compressed into the brief and yet pregnant declaration of John, "in the midst of you standeth One Whom ye know not."

In that same fifty-third chapter this suffering One is described as "wounded for our transgressions . . . bruised for our iniquities . . . a lamb that is led to the slaughter," and that conception John gathered up and repeated in his formal proclamation, "Behold the Lamb of God, Which taketh away the sin of the world!"

Finally Isaiah, in the sixty-first chapter, put into the mouth of this self-same Servant of God the words which declared His anointing for the carrying out of the Divine purposes. "The Spirit of the Lord God is upon Me," and this is exactly what John declared was the specific revelation granted to him, identifying Jesus of Nazareth as the One Who "should be made manifest to Israel," in the words,

22

" I have beheld the Spirit descending as a dove out of heaven; and it abode upon Him."

Thus, before commencing to record the words and works which constitute the media through which God manifested Himself in Jesus of Nazareth, the evangelist has set the whole revelation in the light of the ancient Hebrew economy. Out of all its highest hopes and aspirations there came at last "the voice" which interpreted the meaning of the past, and indicated the fulfilment of all in the Person of Jesus, Who essentially, was the Word, and evangelically, the Word made flesh.

b. THE FIRST DISCIPLES.   i. 37-51

   1. Andrew and another.   37-40

     (? John.) Going from John.

       α. Aroused by John.

       β. Inquiry as Disciples.

       γ. Christ.

          Turned.

          "What seek ye?"

          " Come and ye shall see."

   2. Simon.   41-42

     Called by Andrew.

       α. Simon appealed to by " Messiah."

       β. Christ.

          Looked.

          Defined Present.

             Future.

   3. Philip.   43-44

     Called by Christ.

         "Findeth."

         "Follow."

   4. Nathanael.   45-51

     Called by Philip.

       α. Nathanael.

          Interest.

          Incredulity.

          Investigation.

       β. Christ.

          Definition.

          Revelation.

       γ. Nathanael. Confession.

       δ. Christ. Promise.

b. THE FIRST DISCIPLES

In this section we have the account of the very first things in the public ministry of the Word. In our last study we noticed the close relationship between His Baptism, Temptation,—neither of which is chronicled by John,—and the herald's proclamation,—which is given only by John.

Here we see Jesus with His face set toward His great work of manifesting His Father in the world.

As He went forth, a little group of five was at once gathered about Him, and John gives the account of their finding and following. It is of interest and importance that the relation between this story and those of the calling of these men to service, chronicled by Matthew, Mark, and Luke, should be kept clearly in mind. Matthew and Mark both record how Andrew, Simon, James, and John, were called from the actual work of fishing to follow Him along the pathway of service ; and how they left their father, the hired servants, and the boats, in obedience. It is evident that their abandonment of these was not final, for Luke tells how, through a revelation of His power in the line of their daily calling, Simon, James, and John, left all to follow Him. This however, was subsequent to the initial calling of the five chronicled in this Gospel.

The first movement is an account of the calling of Andrew and another. There is practical unanimity of opinion that the other was John himself. He is never referred to by name in his own Gospel, and that reticence would account for the omission of the name here. These two followed as the result of the great proclamation of the Baptist. Their attitude is revealed by their answer to the challenge of Christ. The name by which they addressed Him, "Rabbi," or Teacher, indicated their desire to be His disciples, and their inquiry, "Where abidest Thou?" suggested at once their wish to come into personal and private relationship with Him, and their wholly spiritual curiosity concerning the meaning of John's proclamation. Christ's dealing with them is interesting, as in the course of it we have the first words which John records as coming from His lips. Taken in their largest sense, they are full of interest. The Word challenges men who follow Him, " What seek ye ? " and when they declare their desire to be His disciples He calls them into close intimacy and promises them vision, " Come, and ye shall see." As a revelation of His adaptation of method to individual needs Christ's dealing with these men is most suggestive. They followed Him out of curiosity of the highest and best kind. This He recognised and challenged when He said, " What seek ye ? " and approved and answered when He said, " Come, and ye shall see." This all happened in the morning at about ten o'clock, according to our time, or in the afternoon at four.[1] For the rest of the

[1] Which, depends upon whether John here used the general Hebrew method of reckoning time or the Roman Civil method. Much has been written on the question. Personally I incline to the latter conclusion. Then it was 10 a.m. when they met.

day they were with Him. What a field
for imagination as to what He said to
them, and what a revelation of His
patience! All preparation completed, and
the great work of manifestation commenced,
He paused for hours in quietness with
two men.

Next in order is the story of the first
meeting between Simon and Jesus. This
was brought about by Andrew, and
Simon was attracted by his brother's declaration that they had found the Messiah.
This harmonises perfectly with the general
impression produced by the study of Peter as
he appears in the New Testament. He was
a Hebrew, intimately acquainted with the
writings of the prophets, and most evidently
looking for the fulfilment of the prophetic
promises of the Messiah. Not a word is
chronicled here of what he said to Christ.
All we know at this point is that he was
willing to come and see One Who his
brother believed was the Messiah. Christ's
attitude toward him was indicative of all His
ultimate process with him. John first tells

us that He looked upon him, and the word made use of is one that indicates a penetrating and understanding observation. He then told him the truth about himself, both present and future. As to the first, He made a simple and natural statement: "Thou art Simon, the son of John," which showed the man that he was known, in the common and simple acceptation of the word. The second half of the declaration foretold the future: "Thou shalt be called Cephas." Again the knowledge which we have of this man helps us to understand how such a statement would appeal to him. Strong, impulsive, having at once the capacity for endurance and the elements of instability, this new Teacher declared to him that he would become a man whose only fitting name would be one that indicated stability and strength. Thus Christ appealed to what was undoubtedly the strongest aspiration of this man for himself, and made His appeal in the form of a confident declaration.

Then follows the account of the first man

called directly by Christ to be His disciple. Again nothing is said of Philip's desire or obedience. That he did obey is certain from the fact that he immediately became a messenger to Nathanael, and in such terms as make it certain that he had found the One Whom he had desired. The declarations concerning Christ in this connection are very simple and very sublime. "He findeth Philip" is the statement, and it suggests a set purpose and a definite method. Having found him, He used the formula which afterwards became so familiar, "Follow Me." Thus another was added to the company of arrested and illuminated souls.

The last of the five was Nathanael. There is a touch of beauty in the story of Philip's agency here. When telling of Christ's method with Philip, John declared, "He findeth Philip." When Philip told Nathanael he said, "We have found Him." Both things are always true. In the case of Nathanael three movements are noticeable in his approach. The first is that of his interest. He also was of the number

of those who were looking for the coming
of the One long foretold, and was thus immediately arrested by Philip's declaration.
The second is that of his incredulity, and is
revealed in his question, "Can any good
thing come out of Nazareth?" The third
is that of his investigation. He was quite
willing to accept Philip's invitation, and
see for himself, in spite of his prejudice
against Nazareth. Christ's method with
him was that, first of all, of revealing His
knowledge of him. He described him as
"an Israelite . . . in whom is no guile," in
which description there was an evident
allusion to Jacob, who had received the
great name Israel, but had been a man
of guile to the end. Here was one who
bore the name worthily. Nathanael's
answering question is a revelation of the
guilelessness of the man. He did not pre-
tend to deny the accuracy of the description,
but inquired, "Whence knowest Thou
me?" Christ then gave him a revelation
of His own knowledge, which answered all
Nathanael's inquiry. We have no means

of knowing all that was conveyed to
Nathanael by the declaration, " Before
Philip called thee, when thou wast under
the fig-tree, I saw thee." It is, however,
most probable that some special spiritual
experience was referred to, and Jesus gave
him to understand that He was acquainted
therewith.

Immediately the guileless Israelite sur-
rendered in words which are in perfect
keeping with that description of him. He
gave Jesus a threefold title : " Rabbi,"
by which he yielded to Him as a disciple ;
" Thou art the Son of God," in which he
recognised the fulfilment of prophecy concerning the Person of Messiah ; " Thou art
King of Israel," in which he recognised the
fulfilment of all Hebrew aspirations in the
Person of Jesus. That confession Christ
answered by promising him yet more
wonderful revelations, and with fine fitness
followed the line of His first description of
Nathanael in which He had made allusion
to Jacob, by declaring to him that the
ancient vision would have spiritual fulfil-

ment in his own experience through his submission to Messiah. It is interesting to note that the title He chose for Himself was that of the " Son of Man."

In this section the interrelation of the coming of Andrew and Simon, of Philip and Nathanael, is full of suggestiveness. Andrew was directed to the Christ by the proclamation of the herald. Simon was brought by the testimony of Andrew. Philip was found by the Lord Himself. Nathanael was attracted by the testimony of Philip. Thus in four distinct ways, in this very earliest movement, were different souls first attracted toward the Christ.

There are also other matters which should not be lost sight of. There is first, that of the first things of the Christ as revealed in His dealings with these men, His first words already referred to in connection with the coming of Andrew and John. Then His first method with one individual, as revealed in His dealing with Simon. Then His first finding directly o a man, and the formula in which He called

the soul into relation. Finally, the first in-
stance in which a detailed account is given
of how He fulfils all the highest aspirations
resulting from the ancient economy.

Then also, there are the descriptions of
Christ given by these early confessors.
He was spoken of as " Rabbi," " Messiah,"
" the Son of God," " the King of Israel ";
and all these descriptions were the direct
results of personal contact with Him. Thus
the truth concerning Himself was breaking
upon the consciousness of these men, and
preparing them for its interpretation with
regard to the revelation of the Father in
subsequent movements.

In connection with this section the student
will find it of great interest to follow the
history of these men. In doing so John
may be omitted, as not definitely mentioned.
Andrew was called to service from the midst
of his life as a fisherman, was present in
the house of Simon when Jesus healed his
mother-in-law, was sent forth as one of
the twelve apostles, at the feeding of the
five thousand introduced the lad who had

the loaves and fishes, was one of the four
who asked an explanation on Olivet of
words of Jesus which gave rise to the Olivet
prophecy, was the one to whom Philip came
when the Greeks desired to see the Lord,
and finally is seen in the upper room on
the day of Pentecost, where he heard the
brother whom he had led to Christ, preach
so that thousands were brought to Him.

The history of Simon is so well known
that only the outstanding events need be
mentioned. His call was a threefold one;
that chronicled in this story; then to service
twice over, as recorded first by Matthew
and Mark, and then by Luke; and finally
to apostleship. The great crises in his development occurred at Cæsarea Philippi;
at the Transfiguration; at the time of his
denial; and in his restoration. The con-
summation of the Master's process with
him came at Pentecost, and was manifested
in his work afterwards, and in the letters
which he wrote.

Philip was called to the apostleship, was
present at the feeding of the five thousand,

and there manifested his calculating ability and the imperfection of his apprehension of his Lord. He is next seen when the Greeks desired to see Christ; and at the paschal board he uttered his own and humanity's need when he said, "Show us the Father, and it sufficeth us;" and he also is finally seen in the upper room.

Nathanael, who, there can be little doubt, was identical with Bartholomew, was sent forth among the apostles; was one of the seven on the sea-shore in the morning of Christ's restoration of Peter; and he too is last seen in the upper room on the day of Pentecost.

ii. THE MANIFESTATION

The testimony of the herald having been borne, and Christ having gathered around Him His first group of disciples, He immediately proceeded to the mission of manifesting God in the world. This mission the evangelist illustrates by grouping works and words in three movements : first, initial signs and wonders of the earliest days ; then the outstanding events and teaching of the formal showing ; and finally, the last sign, in the raising of Lazarus.

a. INITIAL SIGNS AND WONDERS

These have to do with Life and Light, and move in an interesting circle. The first sign was that of life in its creative power. This was followed by the wonder of light upon worship, manifested in Jerusalem, first in the cleansing of the Temple, and then in the instruction of a man. At this point the evangelist introduced the double witness of John the prophet, and of himself, John

39

the apostle. The former is the last voice
of the old, and is a recessional. The latter
is the experimental declaration of the
new, and constitutes a processional. Then,
working backward, he gave the wonder of
light concerning worship in the instruction
at Samaria; and returning to Cana, described the second sign, of life operating in
restoration.

1. *The First Sign.* Life

The occasion of the beginning of the
signs of the Word was a festive and
social gathering. Jesus and His disciples
were bidden as guests to a marriage feast
in Cana. His mother's simple statement,
"They have no wine," in the light of
His reply to her, reveals the fact that
she expected Him to make some manifestation of that mystery of His nature
which she knew, and had kept as a secret
in her heart. His reply was most significant.
Couched in terms of perfect courtesy, He
nevertheless indicated His separateness from
her by addressing her, not as Mother, but

as " Woman ; " and declared that His hour was not yet come.

This is the first evidence of His consciousness that the culminating work of His mission would be accomplished by the Cross. Repeatedly through the Gospel something akin to this is repeated.

Her submission to His rebuke, and her unshaken confidence in Him, were manifested in the word spoken to the servants, "Whatsoever He saith unto you, do it." Then with quiet dignity, He put forth His creative power by turning water into wine, and thus immediately accomplishing natural results ordinarily obtained through slower processes. The ruler's testimony to the excellence of the wine constituted an unprejudiced witness to the perfection of His work. The evangelist is careful to declare that the issue of this sign was the manifestation of His glory, and that His disciples believed on Him.

By this sign essential truths concerning Him were made manifest. First, it was revealed that He had creative power.

By a volition, without a spoken word, He carried processes of nature which usually occupied at least a year, to completion in a moment. Wine in its purity is the juice of the grape, and nature, through its gentle and mighty working, makes this of water. The Lord of nature carried out the process immediately.

The miracle was secondly, a sign that the exercise of that power was at His own personal discretion. His address to His mother showed that the days in which He could act upon suggestion from her were passed.

Thirdly it was made clear that His power would be exerted in answer to faith. When she no longer suggested a line of action to Him, but in perfect confidence told the servants to obey Him whatever His commands might be, He responded.

Finally, this first sign demonstrated His readiness to come into the gladness of human life and enrich it. Many subsequent evidences of His readiness to deal with sorrow were granted. He began with a demonstration of His attitude toward pure joy in the actualities of human life.

2. *The Wonder.* LIGHT

The next sign was in Jerusalem. After a few days' retirement in Capernaum, Jesus went up to the city, and there gave a first public manifestation of His official position. It was fitting that this should take place in the capital, and in the Temple which was the very centre and heart of the national life. The outer courts had been turned into a veritable market-place, with the avowed object of making worship easy by providing sacrifices on the ground. He saw that the motive behind the market was the selfishness of those who wished to enrich themselves; and also, that the effect on the worshippers was evil. Sacrifice made easy is no longer sacrifice; it is superstition. The motive of His action was manifest in His words, "My Father's house." In that brief description is revealed His vision of the Divine purpose and intention in the construction and maintenance of the Temple. It was to be the place where men found their home in the presence of God ; and the prostitution of it to uses which ministered to selfishness, both in the case of the buyers and sellers, violated its original purpose. His method of dealing with such evil was symbolised in the scourge which He made.

The unreasonableness of the opposition offered to Him was immediately manifested in that they asked Him for a sign to prove a sign. The fact that one Man had been able at will to rout the money-changers was in itself a most remarkable evidence, but they challenged Him for a sign to prove His authority to do this humanly impossible thing. He answered in words which at the time none understood, but the meaning of which was made clear to His disciples afterwards. That answer, as He intended it, declared that His cross and resurrection vindicated His authority for exercising His power. Against the making easy of sacrifice, which was resulting in spiritual death, He acted upon the basis of His coming sacrifice at infinite cost, through which He would open the way to larger and fuller life.

This cleansing of the Temple naturally drew attention to Him. It is evident, moreover, that while in the city He wrought more signs, which served further to arrest and arouse the public interest. This interest culminated, in the case of many, in belief " on His name " ; that is, in an acceptance of His claim of Messiahship, which was begotten of signs which gave promise of the fulfilment of their ideas of what Messiah would do. He, knowing the faultiness and imperfection of these ideas, and consequently, the faultiness and imperfection of their faith in Him, could not trust them. The faith in which Christ has faith, is that which is centred on Himself, and so is prepared to follow Him without question, rather than that which follows so long as He seems to fulfil prejudiced hopes.

John then records how, after the shining of the light upon the Temple. and in the presence of the multitudes, it shone upon the life of one man, Nicodemus. He seems to have been one of the finest products of Judaism. In times character-ised by insincerity, and satisfaction with externalities in matters of religion, he was a thoroughly sincere soul, and an earnest seeker after truth. Moreover, in a day when individual thinking was largely in-fluenced by popular opinion, he was deter-mined to investigate for himself, and at first hand; and so came to Jesus by night, not because he was cowardly, but because it was the time of quietness, when he would be likely to obtain a lonely and personal interview.

It was to this man that the Word uttered the truth of the necessity for the new birth. To one who was familiar with all the past, great and wonderful as it was, Jesus was careful to point out that His coming marked the beginning of a new order, and demanded therefore new capacity. All the former had indicated and prepared for the Kingdom, to see and

enter which, in the era of new realisation,
life is required. This life was His own,
soon to be liberated by the mystery of
His lifting up, and communicated to
believing souls. Through the agony of
God's love, light and life were to come
to men.

The conversation fell into three movements. In the first Nicodemus made a
great admission when he addressed Jesus
as " Rabbi," and confessed his conviction
that He was a Teacher come from God.
Christ's answer to that admission was the
simple and startling revelation that in
order to see—that is, to have the first
perception of the kingdom of God—new
life was necessary.

In the second movement Nicodemus
declared his difficulty. His question,
" How can a man be born when he
is old ? " is not as material as it seems.
He simply stated, in material language,
the difficulty of reconstructing a personality. The thought in his question is
that of the unity of the individual, the

relation between all that a man is, and his
physical life, and indicated what seemed
to him to be the impossibility of getting
rid of the past in any new start. Christ's
answer indicated a double necessity. A
man must be born of water and the Spirit ;
that is, there must be all of repentance,
symbolised in that baptism of John which
Nicodemus and the men of his time had
been made familiar with ; but there must
also be that new work of the Spirit which
the herald had foretold would be the special
work of His own mission. Thus, for
entrance to the Kingdom there was needed
not merely all the activity of that life of
which Nicodemus thought when he spoke
of being born a second time, but supremely
a new activity resulting from the work of
the Spirit.

Recognising the difficulty, and the con-
sequent marvel created in the mind of
His hearer, Jesus illustrated the process
by referring to the blowing of the wind.
That may be heard, but cannot be explained.
There are demonstrations of its blowing

which nevertheless, do not explain the whole mystery. As men obey the revealed things of the wind, and so appropriate the power of the unrevealed mystery; so in order to the birth of the Spirit, men must obey the revealed things, and thus appropriate the power of the hidden mystery.

In the third movement the question of Nicodemus was of the nature of an inquiry more than the statement of a difficulty. As the first question really meant, How can these things be possible? the second intended, How can these things be brought about? Jesus again recognised the difficulty, and first declared that the things He had spoken were earthly things, the manifest things, made for man's understanding; and indicated that the heavenly things, the very mystery behind, could not be understood, even though He told them. He then practically claimed to be able to speak the heavenly things, as being the One Who had descended out of heaven; and finally, in a simple illustration drawn from the Old Testament writings, answered

Nicodemus' inquiry. By the lifting up of the Son of Man, life would be placed at the disposal of such as believed in Him.

The paragraph beginning "For God so loved the world" is held by some to be John's exposition of the teaching of Jesus, and by others to constitute Christ's own exposition of what He had already said. Without entering into the discussion, and recognising that in either case we have the Spirit's own teaching, I am constrained to say that I personally believe that these were all the words of Christ. In them the three great facts which He came to manifest are included. Proceeding from the love of God, life and light are placed at the disposal of men. Light creates human responsibility. Through refusing it, man places himself under judgment. Obeying it, he shares the life, through the matchless grace of the giving of love.

3. *The Witnesses*

After these initial signs of life and light, the evangelist records the twofold witness of the herald, and of himself. Having manifested Himself in Jerusalem and in the Temple and to one representative man, Jesus left the city for the country, where He exercised a joint ministry with John; that is to say, He preached repentance and the Kingdom of God, and through His disciples, baptized.

There was evidently an intimate connection between the fact of this ministry and the dispute which arose between John's disciples and a Jew. The details of this dispute are not given, but the outcome of it was that his disciples came to John, and in what were evidently tones of complaint, told him of the great success attending the ministry of Jesus. This was the occasion of the final testimony of the herald to the Messiah. That testimony is the last and highest word of the

53

old economy, and constitutes its fitting recessional.

The apostle of the new economy continues the witness in such close connection that some have treated this whole passage as being the testimony of John the Baptist. It is far more likely however, that this latter portion consists of the apostle's exposition of the final words of the prophet, and constitutes a remarkable setting forth of the principles of the new, and is thus a processional, introducing all that is to follow.

In answer to his disciples, John the Baptist first stated a principle, revealing his recognition of the Divine authority of his own mission, and that of Jesus, when he said, " A man can receive nothing, except it have been given him from heaven." This conception created his content in the accomplishment of his own work as manifested in the success attending the ministry of Jesus. He made application of the principle to himself, by reminding them that they were witnesses of the fact that he had declared that he was not the Christ, but that he was sent before Him. This he had received from heaven. He then made application of it to Jesus in a word which reveals his familiarity with the highest thought of the prophets who had preceded him. " He that hath the bride is the bridegroom." Ezekiel, Hosea, and Malachi had made use of this figure of relationship between Jehovah and His people, and no word John uttered more clearly sets forth his profound sense of the dignity and glory of Jesus than this in which he refers to Him as the Bridegroom, and sees in the gathering of the people to Him the fulfilment of the ancient suggestion that the people of Jehovah stand in relation to Him as Bride to Bridegroom.

In the light of this clear vision he then declared his own satisfaction. His hope was realised. As " the friend of the Bridegroom " he had introduced the bride to Him. It is interesting to remember that Rabbinical interpreters taught that the statement in Exodus, " Moses brought forth the

people out of the camp to meet God "
(Exod. xix. 17), suggested his action as
the friend of the Bridegroom, leading forth
the bride to Him, the Bridegroom. The joy
of the herald was thus fulfilled in the
fulfilment of his mission, and therefore he
was content to decrease in the presence of
the increase of Jesus. There is no touch
of jealousy, no latent sorrow at his own
passing. The tone was triumphant and
glad.

Those who find their true place of service
as God has willed it, rejoice not only in its
greatness and its exercise ; but equally in
its ending, for they know that that which
follows includes all of value, and such
decrease in human service is only increase
in Divine accomplishment.

The witness of the apostle consisted of
a commentary upon that of the prophet,
and was intended to show how reasonable
and right was the position taken. He
first placed John and Jesus in contrast,
not to the disparagement of John, but to
the establishment of the truth of what

he had declared as to the superiority of Jesus.

The term "of the earth," exactly describes the origin, limitation, and message of the Baptist. It is not a term of reproach, but of accurate description. In a conversation with Nicodemus, even Jesus had spoken of all that He had been able to say to him, up to a certain point, as "earthly things." The ministry of John was of the earth in that sense.

In striking contrast, revealing infinite superiority, Jesus is described as "from heaven," "from above." This description must be explained in the light of the opening declaration of the Gospel concerning the Word becoming flesh.

The subject, then, of the new message was that of the testimony of the Word to "what He hath seen and heard." Westcott draws a distinction between the tenses; "hath seen," and "heard," not "*hath heard.*" In all probability there is a distinction in intention. The things seen were the eternal facts which the Word from the beginning knew in fellowship within the unity of Deity. The things heard were those of the great evangel which He was present in the world to proclaim.

The parenthesis of the apostle, "and no man receiveth His witness," stands in striking contrast to the declaration of John's disciples, "all men come to Him," and reveals the apostle's spiritual discrimination between the gathering of the multitudes and their profound acceptance of the witness of the Word. It is in perfect harmony with the declaration concerning Jesus and the men in Jerusalem who believed on His name, but to whom He did not commit Himself.

That this parenthetical exclamation was not to be taken with absolute literalness is proven by the fact that he immediately recognised that there had been those who received His witness, and declared that the issue of such reception was their conviction that God is true. The word "true" here, does not stand in contrast to visionary or imaginary, but to false or lying. The new message, then, which the Word delivered was one which if received, brought the conviction to the soul, that in spite of all the perplexities and disappointments of the past, God is true in Himself, and in His dealings with man.

He then proceeded to emphasise the Divine authority of the witness to Jesus. That consisted, in the first place, in the fact that the words He uttered were the words of God, and secondly was manifest by the fact of the fulness of the Spirit which He bestowed.

The Revised Version here, in the substitution of the pronoun " He " for the word " God," and the omission of the words " to Him," is true to the original text. There is still a difference of interpretation as to the meaning of the statement, " He giveth not the Spirit by measure "; some holding that the teaching is that God did not give the Spirit by measure to Jesus. But the declaration harmonises more perfectly with the subsequent teaching of

Jesus if we understand this passage to mean that through Him the Spirit would no longer be given by measure, but in fulness.

The secret of the authority of the message of the Word lay in the fact of the Father's love for Him, and His having committed all things, including the Spirit, "into His hand." This declaration that all things were given into the hand of the Son does not mean merely for His possession, but for His disposal and administration.

Finally, the apostle declared the nature of human responsibility in the presence of this message of the Son. Such as believe on Him have age-abiding life. Such as obey Him not, do not see life, but remain under the wrath of God. Two things are to be specially noted in this declaration of human responsibility. First, that the words have no application to those who have not heard the witness of the Son; and secondly, that the word indicating the attitude which excludes from life is not the same as the word which indicates the method of entrance into life ; and the Revisers have correctly rendered it, "obeyeth not," rather than believeth not. There is, of course, intimate relation between them. Those who believe always obey, and therefore the disobedience which excludes from life is the active manifestation of unbelief.

4. *The Wonder.* LIGHT

John now presents us with two other initial signs of light and life. Before examining them in detail, it is well to notice how they stand over against the former two in contrast, and yet as complementary in setting forth the fulness of the meaning of the mission of the Word. The first sign was of life acting in creative power. The first wonder was of light on worship in the Temple at Jerusalem, and in the instruction of a man who was a ruler among the chosen people. The second wonder was of light on worship, but in Samaria, apart from any set place of worship ; and of the restoration of a woman who was a Samaritan. The second sign was that of life acting in restoring power.

The incident of the Samaritan woman is full of suggestiveness. In His dealing with her Jesus overstepped the narrow boundary of Hebrew prejudice. " He must needs pass through Samaria." Geographically that was the nearest way, but there is a far deeper meaning in the statement than that. The feeling between Jews and Samaritans was such that the former constantly crossed the Jordan twice, going far out of their way to escape any contact with the latter. This mutual attitude is revealed in the explanatory declaration of John, "Jews have no dealings with the Samaritans." The mission of the Word was opposed to all such narrowness, and in order to find one sinning woman of the Samaritan people, He took the straight course through Samaria. His appeal to the woman for water, was based upon their common humanity. His offer of living water to her, was a revelation of God's attitude toward those outside the boundaries of the chosen people. He indicated His ability and willingness, and suggested the value of His gift, under the figure of living water, able to satisfy, and unfailing in supply.

Having thus succeeded in arousing in the woman interest in Himself, He proceeded with infinite delicacy and precision to the

work of moral investigation, thus bringing her
to an understanding of the reason of the un-
satisfied thirst in her own life. He uttered
one word of command, and she stood face to
face with certain facts in her own history
which she was not prepared to confess, and
her answer therefore was ambiguous, and
might have deceived any but Jesus. He
then told her what she was endeavouring
to hide from Him. Thus He revealed to
her, not her sin, but the fact that it was
known to Him, and so still further fastened
her attention upon Himself. She immediately, from what motive need not be
discussed, submitted to Him a problem
concerning worship, showing that He was
surely compelling her thoughts from things
material to things spiritual.

Thus to a woman, a Samaritan, and a
sinner, He revealed the profoundest things
concerning worship, declaring that true worship is " in spirit." Her outlook had been
a materialised one, and her only difficulty a
choice of place, a controversy as between
the Samaritan mountain and the Jerusalem

Temple. The Lord declared to her that neither place was necessary to worship. This revelation was the statement in word of that which His presence in the world would make real to the experience. When ultimately the veil of the Temple was rent in twain from top to bottom, the holy of holies was not desecrated, but the whole earth was admitted to the inner shrine of Divine manifestation; and to-day, whether in cathedral, conventicle, or cottage, whether in the assemblies of the saints or in the midst of the rush of life on city highway, the soul worshipping in spirit and in truth is accepted in the name and merit of the one abiding Priest.

In all probability the woman did not understand the tremendous significance of the things Christ said to her, but she uttered, perhaps unexpectedly to herself, the subconscious hope, even of the Samaritans, of the coming of Messiah; and straightway He stood before her confessed as that One. That she forgot the lower in the higher is revealed in the fact that she left her waterpot, and called others to consider this great possibility.

The issues of this revelation are set forth in the account which John gives of the return of the disciples. They marvelled to see Him talking with a woman, and, without referring thereto, endeavoured to persuade Him to eat. He then made revelation to them, of Himself, of the present opportunity, and of their responsibility. Of Himself He declared, "I have meat to eat that ye know not. . . . My meat is to do the will of Him that sent Me, and to accomplish His work." In the light of what He had been doing, how gracious were those words ! Breaking through all traditional barriers, and ignoring the conventionalities, He had sat upon the well, and patiently wrought to win one poor bruised soul, that of a sinning Samaritan woman, back to higher things, and He had so far succeeded that even then, as He talked to His disciples, she was on an errand that proved the new interest of life that possessed her. That was meat to Him, for that was His Father's will. Did they, the disciples, desire that bread of deepest sustenance? They might have it to the full, for the fields were white to harvest. It was no mere chance choice of a figure, that reference to whitened fields, yielding the bread of life to men who were offering Him material bread. The chief value of the declaration is its revelation that everywhere souls were waiting for the God Who was seeking them. The disciples' responsibility was created by that wide-spread opportunity. If they would share His reward, let them co-operate in His labour. The work of sowing was accomplished. The harvest was white. They had but to put in the sickle and reap. All this is part of John's teaching of the wide meaning of the work of the Word in the world.

The wonder spread into the Samaritan city itself. So enthusiastic was the testimony of the woman that many believed on Jesus through her word. These came and sought to persuade Him to abide with them, and He did so for two days.

What wondrous days they were for that
community. That He taught them things
even more wonderful than the woman told
them, is evidenced by their final confession, "This is indeed the Saviour of the
world." There was nothing unkind in their
words to her, neither did they discredit
the value of her first testimony. They
evidenced their delight rather, that what she
had first told them was more than corro-
borated by their personal intercourse with
Him. The reception of truth by Samaritan
people was evidence of humanity's readiness for the Word of God, apart from any
privilege of race or caste.

5. *The Second Sign.* LIFE

Finally in this section, we have the story
of the second sign. The opening verses
tell how after the two days' sojourn in
the city of the Samaritans, Jesus returned
to Galilee. There He was received by
the Galileans, many of whom had been at
the feast in Jerusalem, and had observed
the things which He had done. Once

again the working of life is manifested, but this time in restoration.

The incident of the healing of the son of the nobleman is in itself full of beauty. In the coming of this man to Jesus there was manifested first the appeal of venturesome faith. Here was a father whose heart was in anguish because his boy was at the point of death. For the moment his naturally sceptical attitude of mind was overcome by strong emotion, and he besought Jesus to accompany him to Capernaum for the healing of his child. The One Who " knew all men, and . . . knew what was in man," was acquainted with the normal condition of this man's mind, and said to him, " Except ye see signs and wonders, ye will in no wise believe."

Undeterred by the faithfulness of this declaration, and urged by the greatness of his need, the nobleman persisted in his appeal, " Sir, come down ere my child die." That sentence did not prove faith of a high order, but rather determination to make any experiment that might issue in the boy's restoration. Jesus virtually declined to go and create faith upon the basis of a sign. Yet though He knew all the truth concerning this man, He knew also the intensity of his anxiety, and the depth of his love; and so He chose to give him a test for faith, by creating an opportunity for the exercise thereof; and He said to him, " Go thy way, thy son liveth." Thus no sign was given, but a word of power.

In that moment the weak and faltering and experimenting faith which had brought him to Jesus rose on to a higher level as it became obedient. When he made inquiry, and found there was evident relation between the word he believed, and the sign for which he had to wait; his own faith was vindicated, and all his house was won.

The " second sign " reveals the restoring power of the life of God, and shows how that life acts in answer to faith, without reference to geographical nearness or distance.

b. THE FORMAL SHOWING

We now come to the section dealing
with the formal revelation of truth concerning God, through the medium of the
Word. This revelation is developed along
three lines. By works and words, the
facts of Life, and Light, and Love are
set forth.

1. *Of Life*

The Son, in His manifestation of the
Father, is the Source, the Sustenance, and
the Satisfaction of life in the experience
of man.

a. *The Source*

In order to set forth the truth revealed
by the Word concerning the source of
life, John records the work wrought at the
pool of Bethesda, and the words of the
discourse which followed. At this point
began the conflict between Christ and His
enemies which culminated in the Cross.

He had already manifested Himself to representative people at Jerusalem, in Samaria, and in Galilee. No open hostility had been shown. It existed however, and it would seem as though Jesus took action to bring it to the surface, for this miracle wrought on the Sabbath, and giving rise to the first outbreak against Him, was of His own choosing, as to place, and time, and details. From here to the end of the section dealing with His manifestation in the world, the course of this conflict is evident.

The healing of the man at the pool is a radiant revelation of the operation of life in overtaking the results of sin. The opportunity was a superlative one. The man chosen from among the multitude was one who had been " thirty and eight years in his infirmity." It is easy to read such a statement, but it is well to attempt to comprehend its meaning. And yet perhaps that is best done by listening to the answer he gave to the inquiry of Jesus. When he said, " Sir, I have no man, when the water is troubled, to put me into the pool," he revealed the utter hopelessness which possessed him. As a matter of fact, his presence in the porches had become a method of living upon the charity of others, rather than an attempt to secure healing.

Thus the Lord of Life stood confronting the most necessitous case of all the company, and the most despairing one. The initial question of Jesus constituted an arrest of the man's mind, as it brought him back to a consciousness of his real need. It was however, more than that. It is impossible to read the story without feeling that as the words were uttered, a new hope, like a faint flush on the Eastern sky that tells of coming day, rose in the darkened life of the man. Then followed the command, clear, urgent, definite, "Arise, take up thy bed, and walk." Despair had given place to hope. Hope now merged into confidence. Confidence expressed itself in obedience. Obedience was answered with healing.

There can be little room for doubt that these men were familiar with the impotent man. One who had been so long bound by infirmity, and who therefore in all probability was a well-known figure in the Bethesda porches, must have been almost a public character. His healing was therefore a graphic setting forth before them of the operation of life in overcoming the disastrous disability resulting from sin.

Immediately following the miracle the open controversy between the Hebrew leaders and Jesus commenced. Their state of mind is revealed in the fact that the first thing that attracted their attention was not the healing of the man, but that he was carrying his bed on a Sabbath day. Their objection thus in the first place was not due to their antipathy to Jesus, for they did not know that He had anything to do with the matter. It was rather the result of their mechanical and rationalistic ideas of religion. They were shocked by the violation of the Sabbath in so great a degree as to be unimpressed by the wonder of this man's restoration.

These objections Jesus answered, first to the man himself, and then to the Jews. Finding the man in the Temple, Jesus said to him, " Behold, thou art made whole ; sin no more, lest a worse thing befall thee." This was a revelation of the moral meaning of His healing. It is of permanent value, as it shows that whereas out of the pity of His heart He heals men of all physical disability, yet that pity ever operates along the line of absolute loyalty to the principles of righteousness. A man is not healed of those evils which result from sin, in order that he may continue in sin, but in order that he may be strong not to sin.

His answer to the Jews revealed the religious significance of the healing. It was made in terms of brevity and sublimity. " My Father worketh even until now, and I work." In these words He virtually declared that the sin of man had ended the Sabbath, and had brought unrest even to God. From the hour of man's fall God had been at work. In this statement moreover, Jesus claimed co-operation with the Father in His work, and that what He had just accomplished was in immediate continuity of the work of God. Thus He definitely claimed equality with His Father.

The second objection of the Jews arose out of this claim. They distinctly understood it to be that of equality with God. Whereas the violation of the Sabbath had produced objection in their minds which expressed itself in persecution; this claim of equality with God produced feeling which expressed itself in an endeavour to kill Him. It is of the utmost importance to notice this beginning of opposition, and to remember that the final reason of the conflict which culminated in the Cross, was this claim which Christ perpetually made for Himself.

The answer to this objection is contained in the discourse which immediately followed. In that discourse He elaborated the declaration He had made, " My Father worketh

even until now, and I work "; and applied
the claim by showing its bearing on their
attitude of criticism. The co-operation of
the Father and the Son was first set forth in
a new and simple statement, " The Son can
do nothing of Himself, but what He seeth
the Father doing." This declaration denied
His self-determined responsibility for any
thing, and claimed absolute and immediate
Divine authority for all. He then argued
the truth of His statement in a fourfold
declaration, the development of which is
indicated by the use of the word " for."
He first claimed that His own activity
was co-extensive with that of the Father.
He then declared that this extensive activity
was the outcome of the Father's love of the
Son, and the consequent unlimited fellowship existing between Them. He next
affirmed that the evidence of the truth of
these things would be found in His exercise
of co-equal power with God in quickening
whom He would. Finally He announced
that the Father had deputed all judgment
to the Son.

From this fourfold argument He then made His great deduction, that the Father's purpose was that all men should honour the Son, even as they honour the Father; and consequently, that man's responsibility was that of honouring the Son, failing which, the Father which sent could not be honoured.

Upon the basis of that significant claim He described His work as Life-Giver. His general claim was that such as should believe in Him, and hear His word, would have age-abiding life, with the consequent escape from judgment and from death. He then more particularly claimed a present and future exercise of this power of life. He possessed a power which should be manifested in raising the dead, because life was resident in Himself; and ultimately a resurrection of all the dead, either to life or to judgment, would take place in response to His voice.

Such was His answer, and it may be summarised thus, as to its abiding declaration. Because the Word is dependent upon the Father, and acts in perfect harmony with Him, He has unlimited power and authority. "The Father raiseth the dead and quickeneth them," so also does the Son. Therefore the Son represents the Father's honour, and to Him the Father has committed judgment, and the gift of life is also in His right.

Continuing, Jesus called witnesses to the truth of what He had said. Two He refused, and two He accepted. His own witness of Himself He said would be valueless. This is a startling statement, and makes us halt. Yet it perfectly harmonises with what He had already said of His dependence. Lay the stress on "if." "*If* I bear witness of Myself, My witness is not true." This is however, what He disclaimed. He only speaks what the Father speaks, and so the witness He bears is not His, but the Father's. Had His witness been of Himself, then the fact of its being self-originated would falsify it. Thus with uncompromising vigour He forbids self-centred life, and insists upon the God-centred, and makes Himself the Incarnate One, the supreme Revelation of that master principle of life.

John's witness had been to truth. Jesus did not depend upon that, because it was the witness of a man ; and however true it was in itself, might lack that over-whelming conviction which is necessary to the absolute establishment of truth.

In saying that He accepted two wit-nesses, it is necessary to understand that reference is made to the twofold witness of the works, and of the Father ; but because the works are of the Father, the one only witness which Christ accepted was the witness of the Father.

In making His appeal to His works, His reference was not to His miracles save as they were incidents in the whole, but to the great programme of God which He, the incarnate Word, accomplished in His Person and in His work. These works witness to Him because they are the works of God. Therefore the speech of God, not merely concerning the Son, but through the

Son, vindicates the claims of Jesus. Thus with sublime dignity He appealed from self-originated witness of man's testimony, to the works and words of God spoken and accomplished through Himself.

As all this dispute had grown out of the false emphasis of these men in their religious thinking, Jesus now turned back upon them with a criticism which revealed the folly of their position. He declared that their ignorance of God was demonstrated by the fact that they did not believe in the One Whom God had sent.

He proceeded to criticise their attitude toward their own Scriptures, showing that while they searched them because they thought they contained eternal life, yet they would not be obedient to them. Had they been so, they must have led them to Him. Thus they missed the life they sought, because they did not follow the pathway through the Scriptures to the Source of Life, which was the Son Himself. Their dealing with their own Scriptures consisted in a halting with the shell and the shadow, and a consequent failure to find the kernel and the substance.

Continuing, He declared that they lacked the love of God in themselves. This had been evidenced by their having been more conscious of a man's carrying his bed on the Sabbath than of the fact that he was healed. If the love of God had been in them, they would have received Jesus gladly, if for no other reason than because He had healed a suffering and afflicted soul.

He finally affirmed the paralysis of their judgment. They were unable to receive Him, Who had come in His Father's name. Their judgment was warped because they were self-seeking, receiving glory one of another, and were thus unable to comprehend One Who came only to do the will of His Father, and reveal His glory.

Finally, with quiet irony He told them He would not accuse them, but that Moses would, whom they supposed they understood, but of whose teaching as a matter of fact they were ignorant.

β. *The Sustenance*

John now records the signs and discourses which show that the Word is the Sustenance of life, as well as its Source.

In the general scheme of the Gospel the fourth and fifth signs followed each other immediately. The first was that upon which the discourse concerning the bread of life was based. The second was a sign wrought pre-eminently for His own, having a special value for them.

By a comparison of the account of the feeding of the multitude as given by John with the stories of Matthew, Mark, and Luke we discover that it took place after the return of the twelve from their first campaign, and after the death of John the Baptist. Herod having expressed a desire to see Him, Jesus retired across the sea, and withdrew for a while to the mountain with His disciples.

The seclusion did not long continue, for the multitudes followed Him. The difficulties of the situation were many, and those created by the imperfect understanding of Jesus on the part of His disciples are evidenced in the material calculation of Philip, and the faltering faith of Andrew. Christ answered both by action. Taking the simple supply of the lad He made it a sufficient supply for the multitude. The multitudes were so deeply impressed with that wonderful exhibition of His power that they decided that there was nothing for it but to make Him King. This they planned to do by force. He frustrated their designs by withdrawal' to the mountain. This action must have seemed strange to them, and to His own disciples. What explanation could there be of His refusal to fall in line with so spontaneous a movement? The answer is found in the discourse which followed. It may first be briefly stated thus. He knew that the only cause for their action was material. They would fain have as King, One Who could feed them with such ease. He declined the Kingdom so evidently and wholly of this world. He perfectly under-

stood the needs of man's physical nature,
and was able to provide for them, but
that provision was not a sufficiently solid
foundation on which to build a Kingdom.
He turned from such false and worthless
honour to the solitude of the mountain,
and Matthew and Mark tell us He went
to pray. From the lust of materialism
He turned to the strength and satisfaction
of spiritual communion.

The relation of the stilling of the storm
to the general movement of this section
does not appear upon the surface. As
we have pointed out, it was a sign granted
exclusively to the disciples. In all probability His withdrawal from the multitude
and refusal to be made King had caused
His own disciples perplexity and disappointment. They were nevertheless loyal
to Him, He having charged them to pass
over to the other side. In the pathway
of their obedience grave difficulties surrounded them in the coming of the storm.
Suddenly He appeared, and the contrary
wind which hindered their progress afforded

no obstacle to Him, while the waves which threatened to engulf them were the pavement of His feet. Thus He manifested to them His power, even over material things, and so revealed the actuality of His present Kingship, even though He refused to be crowned by men who simply desired to secure One Who with perfect ease could supply their physical wants.

Again the multitudes gathered to Him. They had watched the boats, and had not witnessed His departure, and so were sorely perplexed to find out how He had crossed the sea. He declined to satisfy their curiosity as to *how He* had come, but He told them *why they* had followed Him. Not even the wonder of His working had drawn them, but only their love of food. " Not because ye saw signs, but because ye ate of the loaves, and were filled." Their motive was of the lowest. He called them to the highest ; away from sensual, material ideals, to spiritual. They were seeking meat which perished. Of that He had given them, but His real work was to break to them the bread "which abideth unto eternal life." He urged them to work for that.

Their question, "What must we do that we may work the works of God?" was of the nature of a quibble, and practically challenged His knowledge. When rebuked, human nature has a great habit of affecting ignorance by asking some such question. It is not that the questioners confess ignorance, but in resentment of having been rebuked they challenge the rebuker. Virtually assenting to what He had said, they demanded to know what *He* could tell them about the works of God.

His answer recalled the subject of His previous controversy with them, that of His being sent from God, which was the perpetual difficulty with them. Everything He declared depended, and would for ever depend upon man's attitude toward Him. To refuse and reject God's Anointed was to refuse and reject God, and so to render impossible, works acceptable to Him. Therefore on the positive side, to believe on Him was to make possible the pathway of obedience, so that all life might be the work of God. As unbelief had ever been the all-inclusive sin, issuing in varied manifestations; so faith in Him would be all-inclusive rightness, issuing in constant work pleasing to God.

This is a principle of perpetual application. "Works of God" are impossible to unbelief in His Son, both on account of their nature, and of man's inability. Faith in Jesus is the first work, and brings the believer into possession of the force necessary for all the duties the doing of which will please the Father.

It is perfectly evident that these men understood Jesus to refer to Himself when He spoke of "Him Whom He hath sent," for they immediately asked, "What then doest Thou for a sign that we may see, and believe Thee? what workest Thou?" If they were to work the work of God by believing on Him, what work was He prepared to do in order to call forth their belief? They moreover suggested the nature of the sign which would convince them. He had rebuked their seeking material bread, while Moses had given them bread from heaven, which gift was necessarily a sign to them of his authority. The suggestion then was that He should give them a sign in the higher realm of which He spoke. It is impossible to read this without discovering the astuteness of their attempt to place Him in a difficulty. It is almost impossible to think of a sign in the spiritual realm, at once capable of convincing materially minded men, and bearing the same relation to authority in that higher realm, which the giving of the manna did to the authority of Moses in earthly government. But this is exactly what He did. First, however, with a gentle sarcasm He corrected their blunder as He declared that Moses did not give them bread from heaven, thus revealing the fact that even in their interpretation of their own history they were either careless, or lacked that spiritual sense which discovered the action of God. He then declared that His Father gave them the true bread out of heaven, which was not merely for the sustenance of the physical life, but for the impartation of true life. They immediately asked for that bread, and so practically agreed that such bread as He described would be a sufficient sign of His authority to compel their belief.

Having thus prepared the ground, He distinctly and formally claimed to be Himself that Bread in the words, " I am the Bread of Life," thus offering Himself to them, both as Bread and Sign, and claiming with all distinctness of utterance that to come to Him and to believe in Him would issue in perfect satisfaction of the deepest demands of life. What gracious words were these, and how wondrously the centuries have verified them in all their fullness, and yet how slow even His own are to believe and to find all of life and strength in Him.

Continuing, Jesus announced His assurance that notwithstanding the unbelief of these Jews, all that the Father gave Him would come unto Him, and then imme-

diately uttered the gracious words which
have given confidence and courage to all
approaching Him through the centuries,
" Him that cometh unto Me I will in no
wise cast out."

In this twofold declaration the Lord revealed two aspects of one great effect, the
heavenly and the earthly. The heavenly
takes in the whole result, " *All* that
which the Father giveth Me shall come
unto Me." The earthly declares the individual responsibility, and utters the word
creating confidence, " *Him* that cometh
unto Me I will in no wise cast out." To
ensure the carrying out of the heavenly
purpose, and the earthly possibility, He
came. This He announced and explained.
The announcement was made in the words,
" I am come down from heaven not to do
Mine own will, but the will of Him that
sent Me." The explanation was contained
in the double statement immediately following, which corresponded to the twofold
declaration already made. " This is the
will " concerning the "*all*"; and " this is

the will" concerning the "*every one.*" In both cases the will of the Father centres in the Son, and is accomplished through Him. Of the "*all*" given to Him, He is to lose nothing. In Him "*every one*" believing is to have life. Thus man's responsibility as to the source and sustenance of his own life is perfectly clear. It is simply that he should believe on the Son.

Controversy immediately followed upon this discourse, and expressed itself through the Jews, and through the disciples.

The Jews raised two difficulties, the first concerning His Person; and the second, the outcome of His answer to the first, concerning His purpose.

How sense-bound were these men! Still they stumbled in the realm of the sign. They had asked for that wondrous bread of which He spoke, and He offered Himself to them, and this offended them. Their inquiry, " Is not this Jesus, the Son of Joseph, Whose father and mother we know? how doth He now say, I am come down out of heaven?" revealed the fact that they thought they knew the whole truth concerning Him personally. Had what they declared been true, His claim to have come down out of heaven would have been absurd. Their inquiry makes perfectly clear what they understood Him to mean when He claimed to have come down out of heaven. So far, therefore, their difficulty was a genuine one. They were wrong in their premises, and therefore were wrong in their conclusion. Jesus was not the Son of Joseph. All false conclusions concerning Jesus of Nazareth have arisen from imperfect knowledge of Him.

The reply of Jesus was not a defence of Himself, but a revelation of the reason of their blindness. They lacked the light of life, and the reason for that lack He declared, with evident reference to what He had already said, "No man can come to Me, except the Father which sent Me draw him : and I will raise him up in the last day." This declaration is in harmony with what He had declared to Nicodemus in the midnight conversation, "Except a man be born anew, he cannot see the Kingdom of God . . . except a man be born of water and the Spirit, he cannot enter into the Kingdom of God."

These men lacked the life which would have enabled them to understand Him. In view of this declaration of necessity it may be objected that these men had no responsibility. To this possible objection Christ made reply, as continuing, He revealed the method of the Father, and the consequent responsibility of man. All are taught of God, but only those who, hearing, obey, come to the Son. The drawing of the Father is exercised in His teaching. The responsibility of man is that of obedience.

Then, with the insistence which characterised this series of discourses, He declared again the one responsibility, that, namely, of believing. "He that believeth hath eternal life." Nothing can be plainer from these reiterated words of Jesus than the great fact that salvation does not come by perfect comprehension of the mysteries, but by simple faith in the Person of Christ. He then repeated with distinctness, and in varied forms, those assertions concerning Himself which had been made in answer to their request for a sign of the kind which would convince them. First He simply repeated the claim, " I am the Bread of life," and then using their own sign, made an affirmation by contrast. " Your fathers did eat . . . and they died." " This . . . a man may eat . . . and not die." So that the proof of His claim lay ultimately in the life which they would have if they believed on Him.

Then, by an affirmation more full, and a declaration of result, He emphasised His claim, " I am the living Bread which came down out of heaven : if any man eat of this bread, he shall live for ever."

Finally He gave them a gleam of explanatory light in the words, " Yea, the bread which I will give is My flesh, for the life of the world." The word "flesh" here must be related to the declaration made in the prologue of the gospel:

"The Word was made flesh," and refers to the human nature of the Christ. He thus declared that His human nature, in all its force and values, would constitute the food of man in his essential spiritual life. There is no hint here of atonement, but only of the fact that in some way, not yet declared, He would place His human life at the disposal of man ; and that it is of such a nature that he who partakes, not once, but constantly, for the maintenance of life, will live for ever. So far there is no light on the method of the giving, but only a declaration of the fact of the gift.

There was evidently a pause in the teaching of Jesus after these declarations, during which the Jews, who were more than ever mystified, disputed among themselves. In their statement of their honest diffi culty, there is evidence that they had some dawning apprehension of what He was intending to teach. It would seem as though they granted the general idea that the communication of one life to another might be for the sustenance of the one receiving. Their difficulty was now as to how it could be possible for Him to communicate to them His human life. " How can this Man give us His flesh to eat ? "

In answer to this inquiry the Lord introduced a new statement. Not only must men partake of His human nature for the sustenance of their life, they must also drink of His blood. This figure was suggestive of a way into life through death and sacrifice. Here then He not only declared that they must derive life from partaking of His nature, but also revealed the sublime fact that His life would be placed at their disposal through death, and that they must actually partake in the values of that death to find the virtues of that life.

All this the Lord stated in different ways, each repetition adding force to the importance of the teaching. Men have no life in themselves apart from this partaking of Christ. Such partaking provides a life which will issue in final triumph. His

flesh is " true meat"; that is, His nature
imparted is the truest sustenance of age-
abiding life. His blood is "true drink";
that is, His death is the means by which
life is communicated. Partaking of the
true meat and the true drink issues in
abiding union with Christ. Such union
sets up like relationships between Christ
and the believer to those existing between
God and Christ; and so establishes union
between the believer and God. This is
the true Bread from heaven, not the manna
of the fathers.

Surely now we may say in the highest
application what these men said in semi-
ignorance, "Lord, evermore give us this
bread." It is of the utmost importance in
the consideration of our Lord's answer to
the difficulties of the Jews, that we appre-
hend the significance of His reference to
blood. It is sometimes suggested that it
would be perfectly correct to speak of salvation by the life of Christ, rather than by
the blood of Christ; because " the blood is
the life." While the argument is plausible,

it is wholly false. It is perfectly true
that the blood is the life, but if our salvation were by life merely, nothing more
need have been said than that it was
necessary to partake of His flesh, flesh
being understood to stand for His life. The
introduction by the Lord Himself of the
word "blood," reveals the truth that it is
not by life, but by life laid down that men
are saved. We are kept safe in His life,
but that life can be imparted to us only
through the mystery of the Passion, in
which sin was dealt with, which in this
discourse was suggested by the use of the
word "blood."

This fuller unfolding of the way of life
sifted the ranks of those who were following
Him as His disciples. They said, "This
is a hard saying; who can hear it?" The
word "hard" here does not mean that it
was difficult to understand, but objection-
able. It is evident that they had correctly
interpreted the meaning of His teaching,
as indicating the necessity, on the part of
those who came to Him, for identification

with Him in some way in suffering and death, in order that they might enter upon possession of life. Their estimate of His word as a hard one harmonised with their attitude as revealed in all the gospel stories in the presence of the Cross. Christ was conscious of this, and so far from minimising the value and importance of what He had said, challenged them, " Doth this cause you to stumble ? "

Having thus challenged them, He gave utterance to words of which there have been two interpretations. " What then if ye should behold the Son of man ascending where He was before ? " There are those who hold that by this He intended to suggest that there were severer trials for their faith ahead, when they should see Him crucified. This, however, hardly seems to include all that our Lord intended. Whereas the Cross was the way of His ascension, as this gospel of John perpetually indicates, the fact that here He speaks of the " Son of Man ascending where He was before " surely takes in more than the Cross.

The ascension of the Son of Man to where He was before, must include His resurrection and return to the Father. If this be so, the supposition following the challenge was not intended so much as an indication of severer trials awaiting their faith, as of the fact that in the future there would be vindication of faith in His ultimate victory.

All the records show that from Cæsarea Philippi, when He commenced to speak to His disciples of His Cross, He invariably linked the fact of resurrection with that of the Cross, and these words are in harmony with that method. They constituted therefore a gracious aid to these men as they stumbled in darkness; for by them He gave a suggestion of the issue, as He Himself saw it.

Then in one illuminative statement He explained the true value of the whole discourse. " It is the spirit that quickeneth: the flesh profiteth nothing : the words that I have spoken unto you are spirit, and are life." In these words there are two values, the first being that He lifted the whole subject out of the realm of the material, in which both Jews and disciples were so prone to linger; and the second being that He suggested that suffering in the realm of the flesh, from which they were shrinking, was by comparison as nothing with the triumph in the realm of the spirit, and in the power of life to which He was leading them.

In words of startling simplicity He warned them that He knew that there were some of them who did not believe, and yet in His warning there was an element of comfort, as He suggested that His perfect knowledge of them was the reason why He had declared that no man could come unto Him except it were given him of the Father.

Such teaching winnowed the company of His followers as with the wind of God, and some went back to walk no more with Him. This declaration in all probability included some who openly left Him, and others who, while lingering still in His company, yet failed to accompany Him in identification any further along the pathway of His obedience. Seeing this, He gathered the twelve about Him, and challenged them, " Would ye also go away ? " This question was intended as a further sifting of the ranks, for it appealed to their desire, being as though He had said, If you wish to leave, it had better be so.

The faith of these men acted in the right way, as the speech of their spokesman, Peter, reveals. He first indicated the uselessness of going in his inquiry, " To whom shall we go? "; and secondly, the reason of their staying, in his affirmation concerning Christ, "Thou hast the words of eternal life," and in his confession concerning themselves, "We have believed and know that Thou art the Holy One of God."

Notwithstanding this answer there was defection and evil among them, and that by the deliberate choice of the Master. The declaration of this fact was a solemn one. He declared explicitly " One of you is a devil," thus more fully explaining what He had hinted at before, that he could not come unto Him because it was not given him of the Father. This declaration concerning Judas is startlingly significant. Nothing like it was ever said of any other human being. When at Cæsarea Philippi Christ said to Peter, " Get thee behind Me, Satan," it is perfectly patent that He was speaking through the man to the awful personality with whom He had been in perpetual conflict, and who now was making a disciple the instrument of temptation.

In this case, in calm, deliberate, and distinct terms, He declared Judas to be a devil. While conscious of how much difficulty there has been in the interpretation of the story of Judas, I do not hesitate to give it as my profound conviction that here is the key to everything. Judas was the incarnate antithesis of that which was incarnate in Christ. Not only was he chosen, but created as to his humanity, for the carrying out of that principle of antichrist which is of the essence of evil.

What awful majesty there is about Jesus. He stands for truth, and utters it, until He has challenged the belief of all in Himself. Some fail, and leave Him. Some remain, and enter into life.

110

γ. *The Satisfaction*

The last fact revealed in the section dealing with the manifestation of life is that the Word is not only Giver and Sustainer, but Satisfier.

The effect produced by the Lord's teaching is evident in the statement that He " walked in Galilee : for He would not walk in Judæa, because the Jews sought to kill Him." For about six months He absented Himself from Jewry.

The arrival of the feast of tabernacles was the occasion for the coming up to Jerusalem of vast multitudes, for in many respects that was the most popular of the feasts. The attitude of His brethren at that time was that of cynical unbelief. They could not understand His tarrying in Galilee if His claims were what they seemed to be, and they urged Him to action. The opportune moment seemed to have arrived. He might go up with the multitudes, and work some wonder in Jerusalem, which would fix attention upon

111

Himself, and enable Him to make His
claim, and lead a popular rising. His
answer to their appeal revealed His consciousness that all human impatience and
haste were contrary to the Divine purpose.

At last He went up secretly, and it
would seem that, having reached Jerusalem,
He still evaded observation for some time.
His fame however, had spread so far that
the Jews were everywhere looking for Him,
as He was at that time the chief Object
of interest in the popular mind. Opinions
were divided, some maintaining that He
was a good man, others that He was
leading the multitudes astray. All this
discussion concerning Him was carried on
in whispers, and constituted an under-
current of agitation at the feast. This
revelation of popular interest in Jesus is
in harmony with all subsequent history.
Whether men understand Him or not;
whether they side with, or are against
Him, this much is certain: He commands
interest, He must be considered.

At the right moment, acting as always,

quietly and yet with splendid courage according to the Divine programme, Jesus manifested Himself in the midst of the feast, when the crowds were greatest, and enthusiasm was at its height. He passed through the places of discussion and debate on the market-place and the street, and proceeding to the central position, the Temple, assumed the attitude of authority as Teacher.

Controversy immediately ensued. It first manifested itself in the difficulty created in the minds of the rulers, by what seemed to them to be the wonder of His attainments. The Man of Galilee stood in the midst of the culture of Judaism, and taught; and the manner of His teaching created wonder. He spoke with the accent of culture. As they said, He had the "letters," and yet He had "never learned."

He accounted for what caused their wonder by declaring that the teaching to which they listened, and which astonished them, was not His, but the very message of God. He then gave them a canon of criticism, "If any man willeth to do His will, he shall know of the teaching, whether it be of God, or whether I speak from Myself." If they would obey, they would discover the Divine authority of the things He taught. This was His perpetual method of proof. Not by argument, or statement of logical sequence; not by documentary evidence of any kind, can the Divine authority of Jesus be demonstrated. That demonstration can come only when the venture of faith is made. The results of obedience are the final evidences of Christianity.

He then proceeded to charge them with violating the Mosaic economy, and inferred that this accounted for their inability to comprehend Him. This He emphasised by an illustration. They sought to kill Him, and He traced the opposition to the miracle wrought in the Bethesda porches on the Sabbath. Yet for the rite of circumcision, not instituted by Moses, they perpetually violated that

114

same Sabbath law. It was a scathing criticism of their inconsistency. They lived in surface appearances, and not in the deeps of righteousness; hence their judgment was false.

Some of the citizens expressed their wonder that seeing that this was the Man Whom the rulers sought to kill, they yet did not interfere with Him. This was wonderful indeed, but to us the solution of the citizens' difficulty is to be found in the fact of His perfect security in His Father's will against all opposition until the appointed moment arrived. Twice the effort was made to arrest Him, but without success. He was in perfect safety in the midst of the powerful and persistent enmity of His foes until His final word had been spoken, and their inward corruption had been outwardly expressed in the rejection of all His teaching, and opposition to all His purposes.

They suggested a solution of their own problem, that the rulers had discovered that He was the Christ. That was only mentioned to be dismissed, for whatever the attitude of the rulers was toward Christ, they declared that they knew all about Him personally, and they knew, moreover, that "when the Christ cometh" there would be mystery concerning Him, "for no one knoweth whence He is." This opinion of the citizens concerning Him, Christ criticised by first admitting their knowledge, and then revealing their ignorance. They thought they knew Him, and He admitted that in some superficial sense they did; and then revealed their ignorance by making a declaration concerning Himself which was apart from their knowledge, and which they would not believe.

As a result of His teaching "many believed on Him," and the Pharisees attempted to arrest Him. Again He declared their inability in the words, "Yet a little while am I with you." He knew that presently they would accomplish their designs, but He did not look at that accomplishment as their victory, but as

the completion of His own purpose. To
the words already quoted, He added, not,
You shall arrest Me, and cast Me out,
but, "I go unto Him that sent Me." His
going would be in the march of His
purpose to accomplish the will of His
Father. To Him, secondary causes were
unrecognised. All the pathway was
Divinely ordained, and none could hinder
the progress. The very methods of their
madness would contribute to His triumph,
and the ultimate loss would be theirs, not
His; for presently they, who were so
impotently anxious to be rid of Him, would
ineffectually seek Him.

During seven days of the feast of tabernacles at the hour of morning sacrifice,
water from Siloam was carried in a golden
vessel, and poured out in memory of the
water which had been miraculously
supplied in connection with the exodus,
and as symbolising the nation's hope of
the fulfilment of the prophecies so often
made, of the pouring forth of the Spirit
of God, and the consequent initiation

of a new era. The carrying of this
water was omitted on the last day, and
the omission was as significant as the
observance, in that it indicated the fact
that the promises had not yet been fulfilled. All this is illuminative of, and lends
deeper significance to, Christ's action, when
standing in the midst of the multitudes
He uttered His great call.

In words that are quite unmistakable,
He claimed the fulfilment in Himself of
all that was symbolised by the river of
the wilderness, and all that had been promised by the prophets. He was the Rock
through Whose smiting there should flow
the river of the Spirit for the satisfaction
of all personal thirst ; and in its overflow
through satisfied souls, for the blessing
of those without. Standing thus in the
home, and at the centre of symbolism, He
called men to Himself, promising that in
Him they should find the fulfilment of
all their hopes and aspirations, for life and
service. That this was the true meaning
of His call and promise is evidenced by

John's interpretation, in which he declared that Jesus spoke of the Spirit, which "was not yet given; because Jesus was not yet glorified."

The profound impression which His words made is seen in the effect immediately produced by them. The multitudes discussed and disagreed. Some affirmed that He was "the prophet," some that He was "the Christ," while others attempted to prove from Scripture the impossibility of the suggestion. The rulers were still plotting to take His life, while the officers sent to arrest Him were so influenced by His teaching that they failed to carry out their orders, and returned with the exclamation, "Never Man so spake."

It was in that moment of crisis, when the very air was electric, that Nicodemus raised his lonely voice on the side of law and order. Over all the tumultuous scene there is manifest the restraining power of God, holding in check all the opposition of men, in order that He might accomplish His work and glorify His Father.

120

2. *Of Light*

The Son, in His manifestation of the Father, is the Essential Light of humanity. In this section this is set forth in a definite claim, and by an illustration.

A doubtful Paragraph

An overwhelming weight of evidence goes to prove that this paragraph was not originally part of the gospel of John. For a concise statement of this evidence the reader is referred to the additional note on the passage, in Dr. Westcott's Commentary on John. While this is admitted, the paragraph remains full of interest. If, as appears most likely, it was inserted by Papias, it constitutes a fine piece of extra-illustration. It is as though he had inserted a frontispiece to the section dealing with light, showing how the ordinary standards of the judgment of sin are set aside in the presence of the Essential Light of perfect knowledge and perfect judgment.

Its placing here is full of interest, and in all probability this actually happened chronologically at this point.

It will be noticed that in the Revised Version the whole paragraph is included in brackets. This arrangement of the paragraph throws light for us upon the loneliness of Christ. "They went every man unto his own house, but Jesus went unto the mount of Olives." He had no home of His own. He was houseless and homeless in the world He made, and among the people He loved unto death. And yet how sacred the retirement. He went to communion with His Father, and on Olivet in splendid solitude He passed the night with God. Nothing is told us of the night, and it is not safe to dogmatise ; but I venture to think that He slept, lulled by the wind that bloweth where it listeth, safe from all intrusion, while His Father soothed His humanity, and in sleep gave to His Beloved. It may be that some will object to this, and claim that the night was passed in watching and in prayer.

Perhaps it was so, but I have other thoughts of the absolute rest of a soul devoted to the will of God.

The scene with the woman occurred in the Temple in the early morning. The woman was indeed taken in the very act; but there are so many guilty of acts, who are not taken. These have no right to exercise the sword of judgment. Undetected crime has no authority to cast stones at crime detected. It is idle to speculate as to what He wrote on the ground, and yet an ancient legend is at least suggestive. It declares that in the dust He wrote some word, or words, by which the men looking over His shoulder and reading, knew that He was acquainted with sins in their own past history which they thought undiscovered. Whether this be so or not, it is certain that in the presence of His challenge, and His writing, they beat a hasty retreat. The light was too bright about them for them to dare to cast stones at the sinning woman. Then in the right of the mystery of atonement,

He did not condemn, but rather sent her forth, charging her to sin no more.

a. *The Claim.*

Taking up again the story of John, we come to the section showing the Word as Light. It is introduced by a definite claim which is splendid in its magnificence. The Word is Light in a twofold sense, essentially, and for communication.

Nothing can be more arresting than the words, "I am the Light of the world." Darkness is everywhere; and men, made for light, are groping in it, asking the way, stumbling over hidden rocks, and plunging into perils of all kinds. In the midst of the darkness the light shines, revealing at once the perils and the pathway. This light is for men but it only avails as they walk in it. That there might be no misunderstanding of His meaning, Christ stated it immediately in another form. To follow Him is to have "the light of life." Himself believed in, His will obeyed, His example followed, then men shall grope no longer in the darkness, but walk in the light.

In the controversy that followed, the Pharisees raised no objection to the claim in itself, but refused to believe it because He spoke of Himself. To this objection He replied that even if He bore witness of Himself, His witness was true, because He knew His pathway, whence He came, and whither He went ; and to follow Him, therefore, was to walk after One Who was certain, and not after One Who was making an experiment. By contrast, He charged them with ignorance. They neither knew whence He came, nor whither He went ; and the reason was that their judgment was materialised.

Again, in contrast to this, He declared that the witness of His life was not a lonely one, seeing that through it the Father Who sent Him bore witness. By quotation from their own law He declared that this double witness had upon it the seal of truth. Ignoring His evident intention, they asked Him, " Where is Thy

Father?" and He closed the discussion in words full of severe condemnation, "Ye know neither Me, nor My Father"; and in the repetition of a superlative claim, "If ye knew Me, ye would know My Father also."

Once again the restraining power of God protecting Him is revealed. Although the words were spoken in the Temple, which had become the centre and home of opposition, "no man took Him; because His hour was not yet come."

It would seem as though the Lord were set upon arousing the consciences of these people, for with startling words He warned them that they would die in their sins, declaring that they were "from beneath," that they were "of this world"; and attracting their attention anew to Himself by putting Himself into contrast with them. He was going where they could not come, because of their sins. He was "from above," He was "not of this world." Thus with warnings and declarations of the high nature of His work, He lured them. And yet they seem to have been far more occupied with the speculative aspect of His sayings than with any application of His sayings to life and conduct.

He then told them of a day coming beyond His lifting up, when they would be compelled to recognise the truth of the claims He had made. In a great statement He laid bare the facts concerning Himself. He worked in perpetual harmony with His Father, and His Father did not leave Him alone. The proof of His union lay in the fact that He did the things pleasing to God. John declares the result immediately following this stupendous claim to be that " Many believed on Him."

This is most remarkable. If we would know how wonderful it was, let us endeavour to imagine any other teacher making the declaration that he always pleased God. Others have been able to say they desired to please, their souls followed hard after God ; but the Word Incarnate claimed not merely desire or endeavour, but actual accomplishment. Such a claim made by any other teacher would inevitably issue in cessation of confidence on the part of those who listened. With Him, even in the atmosphere of opposition and unbelief, it carried conviction to the minds of many.

Turning to those who had believed Him, the Lord declared the conditions of true discipleship as to responsibility and result. The responsibility is marked by the simple injunction, "Abide in My word." The result is indicated first as intelligence, "Ye shall know the truth"; and then as freedom, "The truth shall make you free."

How remarkable, and yet how sublime the law of life herein revealed. It is to be wholly conditioned in His word. Where it is so, there will follow an ever-enlarging capacity for, and apprehension of truth. Abiding in that, will issue in the perfect freedom of the disciple. In this statement there was an inference of the bondage of the people to whom He spoke, which they immediately resented by denying that they were slaves. This denial the Master answered by declaring that all sinners are servants of sin, and that bond-servants have no permanent place in the house. Only the Son Who is free, abides. Thus indirectly He claimed for Himself the position of Sonship, and then declared that by making them free from sin, He was able to ensure their permanence also. They, in turn, repeated their boast of relation to Abraham. He denied their relation because of their actions. Abraham's life had been one of obedience to the Word of God spoken to him. They sought to kill Him because He spoke the truth. Thus the relation of flesh was cancelled by antagonism of spirit.

Rising on to a higher level, they claimed relationship to God, and immediately, in words full of searching power, He declared that there were but two relationships in the spiritual world, and that all men are children of God or children of the devil. Their refusal to hear the Son Who uttered the words of God, proved that they were not of God, and consequently were of Satan.

Evidently made angry by the Lord's classification of them, they retorted in kind, that He had a devil, and after further conversation, proved that they were conscious of the logical issue of all that He was saying to them, by asking Him the question, " Who makest Thou Thyself ? " It was perfectly evident that He was taking some position of superiority to Abraham, and in response to their inquiry He emphatically declared His superiority by saying what must have been a most incomprehensible thing to men who looked upon Him only as One of themselves. " Your father, Abraham, rejoiced to see My day ; and he saw it, and was glad."

In astonishment they propounded their second question, "Thou art not yet fifty years old, and hast Thou seen Abraham ? " His reply constituted the climax of His Self-revelation as to Personality. He distinctly affirmed, " Before Abraham was, I am," thus appropriating a form of speech which indicated His proper Deity. He did not say, Before Abraham was, I was,

That would have marked priority. The
use of the words " I am " constitute a
claim to essential Being, which was the
assertion of permanent existence from
which the time element is eliminated.
There can be no escape from the claim
of Deity as herein set forth. That they
so understood it is evidenced by the fact
that they took up stones to cast at Him.
He responded to their unbelief by demon-
strating His Deity in the act of hiding
Himself, and passing through their midst
unseen.

β. *The Illustration*

The story of the healing of the blind
man is the sixth sign in the series John
employs, and constitutes a special illustration of the truth being dealt with. This
is evidently the intention of the miracle
in the economy of the Word, for He repeated His claim in answer to an inquiry
of His disciples, and before giving sight to
the man born blind.

The first stage in the narrative is full

of interest and beauty. The circumstances
created the opportunity for a new departure
which was most remarkable and far-reach-
ing. His disciples approached Him with
a problem concerning a man blind from
his birth. Some of their conceptions of
life were evident in their question. They
considered that limitation is punishment,
and that punishment is retributive. The
man's blindness proved sin. Their difficulty
was to discover whose sin was so punished.
The form of their question presented an
interesting inference. They seem to have
held a view, not uncommon at the time,
that men had some pre-existence, and
suffered in this life for sins committed
before it began, for they supposed that it
was possible that the punishment of blindness from birth was due to some sin the
man had himself committed. It is interesting to notice that Christ neither denied nor
affirmed that conception, save as He denied
their thought that all such limitation was
the result of immediate sin.

If they came to Him with a problem,

He answered them with a great revelation.
The limitation of life evident in the blindness of the man was an opportunity for
the display of the works of God. Then,
in keeping with the claim of Deity made
but recently to the Jews, He declared,
" We must work the works of Him that
sent Me." The plural " We " in this
connection constitutes His claim of co-
operation with His Father, rather than
suggests His disciples' co-operation with
Him.

The words, " the night cometh, when
no man can work," constitute one of those
remarkable soliloquies of which a few are
chronicled in the gospel stories. For the
sake of argument, omit them, and it will
be seen how the main statement is inde-
pendent of them ; " We must work the
works of Him that sent Me, while it is
day. . . . As long as I am in the world,
I am the light of the world."

This soliloquy—" the night cometh when
no man can work "—is the result of His
onward look to the darkness of the hour

to which He was moving. It would be a night in which God would work alone. Even then He would accomplish through the Word, but it would be a death grapple in the darkness. The works referred to here are evidently those which are displayed in the realm of human limitation, such as that of blindness from birth. He proceeded immediately to that work, and bestowed the gift of sight upon one who had never seen.

Differences of opinion arose concerning the man, and he, beset with questions, contented himself with declaring the fact of his previous blindness and present sight.

The case aroused great interest, and the man was brought before the Pharisees. In reply to their question he repeated the fact of his healing. The envy in their hearts against Jesus is manifested by the fact that they were prepared to discount the value of the miracle, because it had been performed upon the Sabbath day, and to argue from that fact that Jesus was a sinner. They appealed to the man for his opinion, and he expressed it in the simple statement, "He is a prophet."

Calling in the parents, the discussion proceeded, with the result that the Pharisees urged the man to give God the praise, declaring that this Man must be a sinner. It is very beautiful to notice how the man gained strength as he bore his testimony, until at last, with quiet irony, he suggested that their interest might be based upon their desire for discipleship; and finally rebuked their blindness, and proclaimed his conviction that the fact of his healing disproved their contention that Christ was a sinner. This roused all their anger, and they cast him out. His loyalty to conscience and conviction had cost him his relationship as a member of the synagogue, and he was now an excommunicated man.

The history of the blind man moved a step forward, and resulted in a very beautiful revelation of the Saviour's heart, marking a new departure in His method of the utmost importance. Remembering the position of the man as the result of his defence of Christ as against the criticism of the Pharisees; the interest of the Lord in him, and His action concerning him, are alike full of beauty. He heard that he was cast out. He found him. He revealed Himself to him, and received his worship. No man has ever suffered ostracism or excommunication for the sake of Christ but that the Lord has found him; and it may as certainly be asserted that in the finding of such an one by Christ, there was infinitely more than compensation for all the loss sustained.

But the story is of greater importance than this. The blind man was the first of a great company, and the action of Jesus was the institution of a new order. As we have seen, Judaism had criticised Him, debated with Him, and practically already rejected Him. To Him, the rejected One, there came this man, and the Word took His position as the new Centre, and received the worship.

From this point onward, His teaching

and His attitude are in harmony with this action. He immediately declared that for judgment He came into the world. That is not to say that He came to judge the world, but to be the Criterion, the separating One, the One by Whom God would judge ; and He proceeded to explain the statement by saying that the result of His coming would be that those who did not see might see, and that they who did see might become blind. Here He was referring to His miracle, and teaching the spiritual truth concerning it.

3. *Of Love*

The Son, in His manifestation of the Father, acts in the authority and power of love.

The relation of this section to the preceding one must not be lost sight of. It is closely connected with the reception of the excommunicated man. By His reception of his worship, Jesus assumed the position and prerogative of Deity, and immediately uttered a prophetic parable setting forth the meaning of that action. By action and teaching He communicated the fact that His coming meant the initiation of an entirely new order, which would set aside the whole Hebrew economy of worship. The light flashes back upon the conversation with the woman of Samaria, and illustrates the meaning of what the Lord had said to her concerning true worship.

The parable did not enter into any details of explanation, but in general terms outlined the necessity for the new order. The

supreme idea is that of a shepherd and
his sheep. All the other things referred to
are subsidiary, and only gather their importance from the supreme matter of the
Shepherd and His sheep. A fold is mentioned; but it is the place of the sheep, and
under the control of the Shepherd. The sheep
are not safe because they are in the fold, but
because they know the Shepherd and follow
Him. The true way of entrance to, and exit
from the fold is by a door, through which
both sheep and Shepherd pass. Those who
gain entrance by any other method are
thieves and robbers.

In the parable it is remarkable that He
suggested that the function of the Shepherd
is exercised in putting forth His own from
the fold, and then Himself becoming the
Centre round which the sheep gather, as
He goes before them, and they follow.

The final test of shepherd and sheep is
knowledge of each other. The Shepherd
knows His sheep, and knows them by name,
and leads them. The sheep know the
Shepherd's voice and follow, but flee from

the voice of strangers. The terms of value
in the parable are those of "the Door,"
and "the Shepherd," and they suggest
authority and love. The supreme word is
Shepherd, which connotes watchfulness,
guidance, tenderness, defence, and all other
matters which are included in the supreme
word, Love. We are not surprised to read
that "they understood not what things they
were which He spake unto them," because,
as it stands, the parable is mystic, and while
the picture was perfectly familiar to the
people to whom it was uttered, portraying
as it did, the Shepherd function, yet its
application was not easily discoverable.

The "therefore" with which the next
paragraph commences indicates the fact
that the teaching of Jesus following resulted
from the failure of men to understand His
general statement concerning the new order ;
and consequently we find therein a detailed
explanation of that parable. He definitely
uttered His claims, and round them His
whole teaching gathered. They consisted
of the two declarations, " I am the Door,"

" I am the good Shepherd." The first, " I
am the Door of the sheep," He made,
and then emphasised, by the declaration,
" All that came before Me are thieves and
robbers, but the sheep did not hear them";
the meaning of which statement must be
gathered by interpreting the word " came "
in the way in which it is constantly used in
this gospel, especially of the Lord Himself,
Who always spoke of His coming as being
authoritative, and the result of Divine
appointment. All who had laid claim to
such authoritative appointment in the past
had been false, and had failed to establish a
new order.

Entrance upon the new order by way
of exit from the old is through Him. Of
the fold He is the Door. The benefits
accruing to those who enter through Him
are threefold. The first is that of salvation in all the fullness of the term; the
second is that of service conditioned in the
freedom of such as " go in and go out ";
and the third is that of perfect sustenance.
Again He placed the false in contrast with

the true, declaring that the thief comes to
steal, and kill, and destroy. His final word
about Himself as the Door is, " I came
that they may have life, and may have it
abundantly." Thus His sheep are put forth
from the fold, and find their entrance into
the new order by the gateway of new and
abundant life.

He then in a natural sequence uttered
His second great claim, " I am the good
Shepherd," which was at once an explanation and enlargement of the one already
made. To those who listened to Him, the
identity of the Door and the Shepherd
would be immediately recognised. To those
of us who know so little experimentally of
the Eastern shepherd this is not at first
so clearly evident. Dr. George Adam
Smith has told how when in Syria he
came in the course of journeying off the
beaten track, to a fold, in which sheep were
gathered, and over which a shepherd
watched. This fold consisted of a wall
through which an opening served as entrance. In conversation with the shepherd

he drew attention to the fact that there was no door, and received the reply, " I am the door," the shepherd going on to explain that at night he lay in the entrance, so that no sheep passed out, and no wolf could find entrance, save over his body. Thus the Shepherd of the sheep is the Door of the fold.

The first declaration which Jesus made concerning Himself as the good Shepherd was, " The good Shepherd layeth down His life for the sheep." This He explained by contrasting it with the action of the hireling, who, having no care for the sheep, flies at the coming of the wolf, leaving them to be snatched and scattered. The first fact then about His relationship to the sheep as the good Shepherd is that He loves them even to death. For their protection He engages the wolf, even though He dies in the conflict.

This, however, is an imperfect figure. Like all parables, even those of the Lord Himself, the tremendous truth to be taught is so mighty that the figure is not large enough to contain it. In the ordinary

course, if the shepherd die in conflict with
the wolf, even though the wolf be slain, the
sheep are left without a shepherd. Jesus
therefore now repeated His claim, and spoke
of Himself as knowing His own, and laying
down His life for them, which statement in
this case means far more than in the first.
To lay down the life, as we have seen, is
first to die for the sheep; but it is in a
fuller sense to communicate it to the
sheep, so that they may share it. He
immediately therefore, declared His larger
purpose of finding other sheep, "not of
this fold," whom He also would lead, and
at once He made use of the great word
"flock," which very largely cancels the
value of the word "fold." All the meaning
of the new order is summarised in one
brief formula, " One flock, one Shepherd."

At last the word " love " is uttered, and
it is the love of the Father to which He
refers. From the Father He had received
His authority to lay down His life and take
it again. Almost ruthlessly He swept away
the idea that it was possible for men to take

His life from Him, and thus in advance
interpreted the meaning of His dying as
being that of determinate action in fellowship with God, and an expression of that
love of God for Him, which was also and
consequently the expression of the love of
God for those for whom the Shepherd
lays down His life.

In the study of this wonderful passage
it is of supreme importance that we distinguish between the fold and the flock.
The fold is not valueless. It has its place,
but it may be entered and left, according
to the guidance of the Shepherd. The
flock is supreme. The relation of Christ
to fold and flock, moreover, must be borne
in mind. To every fold in which His
sheep are gathered, He must be the Door.
Of the whole flock He is the Shepherd.
Entrance by that door means salvation,
service, sustenance. Membership of that
flock means deliverance from the wolf by
the death of the Shepherd, the Shepherd's
life received, and consequently the Shepherd's fellowship with the Father shared.

There are still many folds. There is but one flock.

It was inevitable that such teaching should issue in renewed controversy. So strange had the words sounded in the ears of those who listened, that many of them declared that He had a devil. Others denied that One possessed with a devil could utter such sayings, or accomplish such a wonder as that of opening the eyes of the blind.

John chronicles the fact that it was winter, and that the Master walked in the sheltered porch of Solomon, a beautiful touch revealing the perfect humanity of Jesus in the midst of teaching that flames with the splendours of His Deity.

The Jews asked for some definite pronouncement. In reply He referred them first of all to what He had already told them, reminding them that they did not believe Him; and then to the works that they had seen, which they also refused to believe. In declaring the reason of their unbelief, in a few words of great beauty

He restated the facts of the new order, first, as to the relation existing between the flock and the shepherd, and then as to the relation between the sheep of His flock and His Father; concluding with a sublime declaration which was the revelation of the authority of His teaching and His action, "I and My Father are one." The reason why they neither believed His words nor works was that they were not of His sheep.

Again their opposition flamed forth. Undoubtedly stung by His interpretation of the reason of their blindness, they took up stones, because they distinctly understood the words He had uttered concerning His relationship to His Father to mean that He claimed to be God. This was declared in so many words in their reply to His inquiry for what good work they stoned Him. By that wonderful power, whose working we have noticed in the earlier parts of the gospel story, they were restrained from the act of stoning Him, while He restated His proof of all

He taught as being found in the works He did. Quoting from their Scriptures, He showed how those were "called gods unto whom the word of God came." If they were so described, was it blasphemy on His part to claim to be the Son of God, when He was the incarnate Word? The proof of relationship for them was to be found in His works. Again we see their impotent rage, and His marvellous power as "they sought to take Him: and He went forth out of their hand."

Once more, cast out by unbelief, there was a repetition on a larger scale of the going out to Him of those who were seeking for truth, and who were sincere in their search. The revelation of love which began with the reception of the excommunicated man, and had been made clearer in the wonderful teaching concerning the new order, was thrown up into sharper relief by the hostility of those who sought to harm Him. Its victory was manifest in the closing words of the section, "Many believed on Him there."

150

c. THE FINAL SIGN

An immediate crisis was now reached
in the ministry of Jesus. John gives a
detailed account of the seventh and final
sign of His manifestation in the world.
While its supreme value is its revelation
of life acting in restoration, the sign gathers
up within itself the three elements of love,
of light, and life.

1. *Love*

The revelation of love is that of the
mystery of its method and the perfection
of its wisdom. In the background one is
conscious of the home at Bethany, with
its atmosphere of perfect human love, the
home in which Jesus had been for long
time the welcome guest, and the trusted
friend.

It was the atmosphere of love which
created the sorrow that filled the hearts
of the sisters as Lazarus lay sick. Their
thoughts instinctively turned to the One
Whom they perfectly trusted. They des-

patched a messenger to tell of His friend's
sickness, being sure of His interest and
His succour.

His reception of the news was calculated
to fill them with amazement. It is some-
what difficult for us to realise this, as the
sequel to His action is known to us. We
must however, remember that it was not
known to them. Evidently He received
the message and understood it, but the
only remark that He made was the
declaration that the "sickness was not
unto death, but for the glory of God,
that the Son of God may be glorified
thereby." Having said this, He tarried;
but John is careful to preface his statement of the tarrying of Jesus by the
declaration that He "loved Martha, and
her sister, and Lazarus." It was because
of their certainty that Jesus loved Lazarus
that they sent for Him; and yet, according
to this statement, it was His love that
made Him tarry. His apparent indifference
appeared to be evidence of lack of love,
whereas it was really the final proof of

His love, not for Lazarus only, but also for Martha and Mary.

It is well to notice at once that the word by which they described and thought of the Lord's love for Lazarus is φιλέω, while the word which John used to declare the Lord's love is ἀγαπάω. Each of these words has been used by John in the earlier parts of his gospel. Here for the first time they come into nearness and into contrast. As in the later sections of the gospel we shall find them together again, it may be well now to pause to distinguish between them. That there is a difference cannot be denied, but it is not easy accurately to define the distinction. Dr. Westcott says that φιλέω suggests personal affection, the feeling which answers to nature; while ἀγαπάω refers to the feeling which comes from reflection and knowledge, and describes the love of experience and judgment. Dr. Strong says that φιλέω denotes personal attachment as a matter of sentiment or feeling, while ἀγαπάω embraces the idea of the judgment and

153

deliberate assent of the will. These defini-
tions will enable us to see the importance
of making the distinction between the
words in this case. The sisters thought
of the love of Jesus for Lazarus as that
of a purely emotional affection, which
would have hurried to be with him.
Therefore John is careful to declare that
the love of Jesus for Martha, Mary, and
Lazarus was that of a strong, intelligent
affection, which was based upon perfect
understanding, and therefore tarried in
order that at last the greater victory might
be won, and a finer manifestation of love
granted.

2. *Light*

At last, in the leisure of this perfect
love, the Lord turned His face toward
Judæa, and therefore toward the sorrowing
sisters; and this was the occasion for His
uttering to His disciples words which
flame with light. They were afraid of the
danger that threatened Him in Judæa. In
quiet dignity and calmness of spirit He

declared, that the day would suffice for the work, that the work was not accomplished, that the day was not yet ended. This is a revelation of His own consciousness of the fact, which we have observed more than once, that His foes were utterly powerless to touch Him until the proper moment arrived.

He then told them that the object of His coming was to awaken Lazarus out of sleep. In these words He revealed His estimate of death for all such as love Him. It is a sleep. His disciples had not yet learned this language, and had no thought that He referred to death, as is seen in their statement that if he slept he would recover. Without any tinge of rebuke He accepted the language of their incomplete understanding, and told them that Lazarus was dead.

Thus they started; He walking in perfect light, and therefore in perfect calmness; they following in love, ready to die with Him, even though as yet the light was darkness to them.

3. *Life*

At last, four days too late, as it would seem, the news reached the house of mourning that Jesus was approaching ; and the first picture presented is that of His dealing with Martha. Leaving the house, she hastened to meet Him, and in the first words she addressed to Him we have a remarkable revelation of her attitude toward Him. Her disappointment expressed itself in complaint, " Lord, if Thou hadst been here, my brother had not died." Her confidence expressed itself in her assertion, " Even now I know that whatsoever Thou shalt ask of God, God will give Thee." Her limitation expressed itself incidentally, but none the less clearly in the words she used concerning Him, "Whatsoever Thou shalt ask of God."

The word " ask " ($\alpha i \tau \acute{\epsilon} \omega$) is a word that Jesus often made use of when speaking of the praying of His disciples, but never when referring to His own praying. It suggests the asking of a favour, while He ever spoke

of His relation to God as that rather of
communion or fellowship based upon perfect
equality.

The Lord however, ignored the complaint and the blunder, and answered only
the confidence of Martha by declaring,
" Thy brother shall rise again." To this she
replied, with evident impatience, that she
knew he would rise at the last day, the
very affirmation of her confidence in the
midst of her grief showing that she realised
that there was little comfort for present
desolation in anticipation of an event so far
postponed. Then the Lord surcharged the
clouds that hung about her with the light
of a new and marvellous revelation, uttering
His great " I am " of resurrection and life.
He asked if she believed. She seemed to
be bewildered, and yet silenced. In her
reply she affirmed the faith she had, faith
in Him, and thus refused to affect a faith
which she did not possess. This faith is
all He ever asks, for even though it cannot
intelligently take hold upon all He says,
it is the very condition of discipleship,

and must issue in the enlargement of faith with the increase of understanding.

If to Martha, filled with feverish perplexity, He gave His teaching and the promise of life ; to Mary, quiet even in the midst of sorrow, He gave His tears, and the activity of life ; thus revealing to her the cost to Himself of the victory to to be won.

Mary had remained in the house until Martha, bearing the message of Jesus, called her. At that call she rose quietly and passed to meet her Lord. Falling at His feet, where Martha had stood erect, she uttered the same words, and yet evidently in an entirely different tone. This is proved by the effect produced upon the Lord, for His method is ever that of replying to what the condition demands. Martha's agonised perplexity called for teaching. Mary's surging but submissive sorrow asked for sympathy, and this was supplied by an unveiling to her of His own sorrow.

Three stages of revelation are to be found in the three expressions, "He groaned in the spirit," " He was troubled," "Jesus wept." The phrase "Groaned in the spirit" is marginally translated in the Revision, " Was moved with indignation in the spirit." In this is revealed in almost startling vividness the passion of God in the presence of the final issue of sin, which is death. It is a word that suggests the mingling of pain and anger; anger at the cause, pain in the presence of the effect. The second phrase, " Was troubled," is again more suggestively translated in the marginal reading " He troubled Himself," and in this is unveiled the voluntary nature of His identification of Himself with sorrow, and ultimately with the sin causing sorrow. This sense of sin and identification with all its issue was at once the secret of His power to abolish death, and the foundation of that perfect sympathy which expressed itself in the tears He wept in the presence of the sorrow of Mary.

At last the final sign was wrought, as, standing in the presence of death, He spoke the word which broke its power, and gave life to the man who for four days had lain within the grave. In that final sign there is a sevenfold process which we do well carefully to ponder. Lazarus was raised, first through suffering, " again groaning in Himself "; secondly, against unbelief, for Martha protested against the removal of the stone; thirdly, in perfect fellowship with God, as demonstrated by the prayer which, as He Himself said, was offered for the sake of those standing around; fourthly, with unquestioning authority, as is revealed in the simple and sublime command, " Lazarus, come forth "; fifthly, in mighty power, for Lazarus came forth; sixthly, to perfection in smallest details, as is shown by His final command to loose him and let him go ; seventhly, with division of effect, for many believed on Him, while some reported to His enemies the things that He had done.

162

iii. EPILOGUE

The section dealing with Manifestation in the World ends with an epilogue, which gathers up in a series of movements the results following the ministry of Jesus.

a. *Illustrations of Results*

The first part of the epilogue is occupied with illustrations of results. His foes plotted for His death. His friends gathered about Him at the social board. The Jews made a public demonstration. The Gentiles attempted to see Him.

The last sign raised the opposition of His foes to the point of definite activity. A coalition was immediately formed. The chief priests, who were Sadducean, and therefore denied resurrection, made common cause with the Pharisees, who while believing in resurrection, were not prepared even in the presence of overwhelming testimony to believe in Him. The cowardice of the opposition is evident in the statement that these men feared that "the Romans will come and take away both our place and our nation." The nation was already groaning under the iron heel of Roman oppression. They had lost in all highest sense both place and nation. They had nevertheless contrived to retain much personal power, and it was this they were afraid of losing. Their cunning was of the worst. There was no true patriotism in their position. They did not at all mind that the people should bend to a yoke, if only they were permitted to help in the driving; but if there should be any possibility of the breaking of the yoke which would issue in their loss of power, that must be prevented at all costs. This explanation of their opposition is based upon their own argument. Their reason however, lay much deeper. It was that of hatred of One Who by word and work had denied the materialism of their religious outlook, and rebuked their degradation of the spiritual ideal.

The statement of Caiaphas that one must die for the nation was cunning, contemptuous, and cruel. Yet with scarcely veiled irony John points out that, being high priest, he uttered a true prophecy. The philosophy of Caiaphas was, that if one man troubles a nation, it is better to kill him for the good of the nation. Like Balaam of old, he uttered unconsciously a profound truth when he said, "It is expedient for you that one man should die for the people." This was the result of the ministry of the Word so far as His foes were concerned. The council decided that His death must be accomplished, and Jesus retired "into the country near to the wilderness," where He tarried with His disciples while the last of the twelve hours of the day was passing, and the night approached.

The shadows of the Passion were falling across the pathway of the Word. But a few short days remained, and then the Cross. Under these circumstances He turned to Bethany and to the companionship of the three He loved so well, Mary, Martha, and Lazarus. The scene at the supper places in vivid contrast the representatives of opposing attitude toward Christ. Mary and Judas arrest our attention. She having become familiar with the place of discipleship and adoration at His feet in days full of sunshine, and having known the power of His sympathy in the hour of her sorrow, appreciated the nearness to her Lord and Master of some great death-sorrow. Passing nearer to that sorrow than perhaps any other, she laid her costliest gift at His feet, the symbol of her loyalty and her love. He appreciated the action at its true worth, recognising the anointing to His burial, and preserving the perfume of the spikenard in such a way that it has made fragrant all the centuries. Judas having utterly failed to understand the Lord, because blinded in his self-interest, criticised the imprudence of the action of a love to which he was an utter stranger, and was rebuked by the One Who valued the uncalculating abandonment of fervent devotion.

The two are types, superlative ones it may be granted, and yet for ever serving as contrasts by which men may try their relation to the Lord. The love which

defies arithmetical calculation is ever breaking some box of fragrant spikenard upon
His feet, and gladdening His heart. The
calculating prudence, which is more occupied
with the gift than with the Lord, ever borders
upon that treachery which may at last sell
Him for thirty pieces of silver, or even less.

From the quietness and seclusion at
Bethany the Master passed to Jerusalem.
Here He was received with a spontaneous
outburst of welcome. A public entry
pre-arranged by Christ culminated in that
great scene which fulfilled the prophecy,
"Fear not, daughter of Zion, behold, thy
King cometh, sitting on an ass's colt." It
was a strange triumph. The disciples did
not understand it, for they failed to link it
with the prophecy until after His resurrection. The shout of the crowd was of little
worth, for the people were swayed by low
motives; and before the sound of the
Galilean Hosanna had died away, the
clamour of the Judæan Crucify had begun.
Nevertheless He moved quietly on, His
heart gladdened, not by the immediate and

worthless welcome, but because He knew that by the very agony to which He was moving, He would ensure another day of triumph, when the shoutings of the ransomed would never merge into the howls of rebellion and rejection.

That is the point of supreme value in this entry to Jerusalem. It is a symbolic setting forth of that perpetual progress in which He moves through the worthless present, transmuting it into the triumphant future. No human failure ever diverts God from the purposes of love. It may be added that no present event can be perfectly understood. Well is it for those who have learned to follow, to trust, to wait.

The coming of the Greeks was to Jesus the symbol of the larger work He had come to do. When He heard of their request He said, " The hour is come that the Son of man should be glorified." By that He did not mean that in that little hour marked by the dial, and because travelling Greeks had asked to see Him, He had achieved a victory.

There was nevertheless the closest connection between the statement and their coming. This title, "the Son of man," of which He was so fond, links Him to the whole human family, and the approach of these men outside the Jewish covenant was to Him prophetic of the gathering to Him of the peoples of all nations and tongues. He was deeply conscious, however, that the gateway of entrance for these was that of His Cross and passion. Through that Cross the Son of man would be glorified, because through that Cross such seekers would find all that they most needed. This surely was the first intention of His words about the grain of wheat. For the Greeks to see Him then, would be to fail utterly to understand Him. He was the lonely seed corn. Presently they would see Him in the glorious harvest following His passing through darkness and death into light and life.

At this crisis He uttered words which reveal His own conception of the necessity for His Cross, of the nature of its experience, and of the certainty of its victories. His soul was troubled, and yet there was a stronger passion in Him than that sense of coming pain. It was His passion for the glory of the Divine name, and therefore He did not pray to be saved from the approaching hour, but that His Father would glorify His name. In answer to that prayer the Divine voice spoke, and upon the authority of the promise made, " I have both glorified it, and will glorify it again," He uttered some of the most wonderful words about the Cross on record, declaring it to be a throne of judgment, a force of eviction, and a centre of attraction.

These words in which there mingled the tones of travail and of triumph, the evident sense of a coming death and an abiding life, perplexed the multitudes, who asked an explanation. He replied by charging them to walk in the light, in order that they might become sons of light.

It is noticeable that the story ends with the words, " Jesus . . . departed and hid Himself from them," thus declining to

satisfy the curiosity of the Greeks until
the work should be complete by which
their deepest need should be fully met.

b. *The Summary*

The epilogue closes with a brief paragraph in which John gives a summary
of result, and of teaching.

As to result, notwithstanding the signs
which had been wrought, the people did
not believe, and this fact was a fulfilment
of the ancient prophecy of Isaiah. In
dealing with the work of the herald, John
the Baptist, we drew special attention to
the fact that he, the "last and greatest of
the Hebrew prophets, had been supremely
impressed with the teaching of his illustrious predecessor, Isaiah"; showing how
this was proved by his own words. It is
of interest therefore to see how at the
close of this first section John the apostle
summarises results by quotation from this
same prophet Isaiah. No worker for God
has ever entered so fully and deeply into

171

that great wail of the old prophet as did Jesus Himself.

" Lord, who hath believed our report?
  And to whom hath the arm of the Lord
    been revealed ? "

John proceeds by another quotation from Isaiah to declare the reason of this unbelief. " For this cause they could not believe, for that Isaiah said again,

" He hath blinded their eyes, and He
      hardened their heart,
  Lest they should see with their eyes,
      and perceive with their heart,
  And should turn,
  And I should heal them."

The first impression made by this quotation is that if God had blinded the eyes of people so that they could not see, and hardened their hearts so that they could not believe, there could be no blame attached to them. But this is to misunderstand the deepest meaning of the

172

statement. The only sense in which it can ever be said that God blinds the eyes or hardens the heart is that revealed in the story of Pharaoh. When man refuses to see, and refuses to believe, he loses the power of sight, and becomes hardened, in the very nature of the case. This is an irrevocable law; and as God is the Author of all law He is said to do what is done naturally. That does not interfere with the fact that He does it through the operation of law.

Thus behind the blindness and hardness which prevented men seeing or understanding Christ, was the sin of disobedience in the presence of previous light, the penalty of which was inability to appreciate the new light.

There was however, in addition to this blind unbelief a remarkable measure of fearful belief even among the rulers. There were those who were convinced, and even though they were afraid to confess, they nevertheless believed. John sets little store by this belief, for he dismisses them with a touch of scorn as he declared, "They loved the glory of men more than the glory of God."

As to the teaching, we have here what is evidently the last public testimony of Jesus. It is very brief but very clear, consisting of a summarised statement of His claims. It was made just as the light of the working day was passing, and the hour of darkness was approaching. This is seen by comparing verse thirty-six of chapter twelve with the first verse of chapter thirteen. "While ye have the light, believe on the light, that ye may become sons of light." Here the reference was most certainly to His own presence amongst them, which was almost at an end: "Jesus knowing that His hour was come that He should depart out of this world." Here John makes a statement that the day's work was nearly over, and that the night was coming. At this point Jesus made His last public statement, which had to do with His Person and His teaching, and the purpose of both.

As to His Person He declared that He was the Light, because He revealed God. " He that beholdeth Me beholdeth Him that sent Me."

As to His teaching He declared it to be authoritative, and that, because it was from God. " The Father which sent Me, He hath given Me a commandment, what I should say, and what I should speak." The issue of the whole is eternal life.

Nothing can be more sublime than these closing public utterances of Jesus. They are in perfect harmony with the marvellous conception of Him presented to us in this gospel as the revealed Love, and Light, and Life of heaven.

II. TO HIS OWN

The second movement in the division dealing with the Manifestation of God, records events and teachings in which Jesus gave Himself exclusively to His own. The essential revelations are the same, but they are now made to that inner circle of believing souls who are able more perfectly to understand the Divine manifestation. It falls into four parts; of which the first is an unveiling of His love as He speaks of Himself; the second is an unveiling of light as He speaks of the Paraclete; the third is an unveiling of life as He speaks of Himself perfected in His own by the Spirit; while the fourth contains the prayer of the Word.

i. LOVE. HIMSELF

The unveiling of love is introduced by a fundamental affirmation, and consists of a supreme act of lowly service, instructions concerning the perfected communion, and a discourse concerning His going.

a. THE FUNDAMENTAL AFFIRMATION

Having turned from the people who had rejected Him, Jesus devoted Himself exclusively to His own in the last hours. This fact John indicates by the declaration, " Having loved His own which were in the world, He loved them unto the end." All that follows results from, and illustrates that love. Jesus knew " that His hour was come, that He should depart out of this world unto the Father," and He gave Himself to that tender ministry of love, in order to prepare them for the days in which He would be away.

b. HIS OWN LOVE SYMBOLISED

In the quiet seclusion of the hours spent with His own, His first act was one characterised by the greatest simplicity, while at the same time it was the most sublime unveiling of the perfection of His love. He knew, as John declares, " that the Father had given all things into His hands, and that He came forth from God, and goeth unto

God." This declaration affords a remarkable revelation of our Lord's contemplation of all that lay before Him. If we have seen in previous studies His sense of the awfulness of the Cross, here we have a picture of the perfect triumph of His spirit over all such sense, in His consciousness of the real meaning of His exodus. He came from the Father; all things were delivered unto Him of the Father; He was going to the Father. There is the ring of assured victory in the whole statement. Having this clearly in mind, His first action becomes the more remarkable. Rising from supper, He girded Himself with a towel, and proceeded to wash their feet. It was the work of a slave, and expressed, as perhaps nothing else could have done, His absolute devotion to His own.

While the self-evident lesson of the washing of the disciples' feet was that of our Lord's humility and abandonment to the service of His own, its particular application was undoubtedly the revelation of the fact that He had made provision for the cleansing

179

of His disciples from defilement contracted by the way. When Peter objected to the washing of his feet the Lord replied, " If I wash thee not, thou hast no part with Me." The whole action was Eastern, and the picture suggested to the mind is that of the Eastern baths. A person having bathed walked to the dressing-room, and in that walk contracted defilement. It was necessary therefore, not again to plunge into the bath, but to wash the feet before adjusting the sandals. This fact illumines Christ's words, " He that is bathed needeth not save to wash his feet, but is clean every whit." By this act therefore love is symbolised in its lowliness, and in the fact that it provides against the failures of His own.

c. THE PERFECTING OF COMMUNION

Having completed the washing, He gave the disciples explicit explanation of the meaning of what He had done. He taught them that the highest act of service that believers can render to each other is that of restoring the fallen brother from defilement contracted in his walk by cleansing through the ministry of the Word. In fellowship with the Lord Himself they are to serve in lowliness, and with the purpose of restoring such of their number as fall. From this sacred fellowship He exempted Judas, intimating to the disciples that one of those familiar with Him would lift up the heel against Him. It is very beautiful to notice His reason for making this reference to Judas at this point, as declared in His own words, " I tell you before it come to pass, that, when it is come to pass, ye may believe that I am." When the events of His betrayal would in all probability stagger them, they would be strengthened by the remembrance of the fact that He foresaw both the betrayal and its method. Thus, as ever, He prepared them for the difficulties to come.

Evil always troubled Christ, and the thought of His betrayal caused Him sorrow, not, as I think, because of the pain that was coming to Him, but because of the evil that was working the pain. He now made the

statement that one of them should betray
Him more emphatic, and privately answering
the question of John, indicated the betrayer
to him alone.

At this point Judas, having received
the sop, withdrew from the company. How
much of suggestion there is in the declaration, " He . . . went out . . . and it was
night." Immediately following his departure Jesus said, " Now is the Son of man
glorified." The night without, the shining
of glory within.

This statement of Christ concerning His
glorification is a very remarkable one in the
light of the going out of Judas. It declares
" the Son of man glorified " in the going out
of evil; and in the fact that evil had gone
forth to express itself in final sin; and yet,
because under the government of God, to
the accomplishment of the Divine purpose.
The Son of man was glorified in the fact
of his exclusion, and in the fact that he had
gone to encompass that death through
which the larger glory would be wrought.

At last He was quite alone with His

own, and immediately laid upon them the one law of love. The uttering of this commandment at this point serves to emphasise it. The law of life among the disciples is to be that of love like that of their Lord, and, consequently, utterly unlike the action of Judas.

d. CONCERNING HIS GOING.

The exclusion of Judas made possible the final instructions of Christ to the immediate circle of His disciples. In laying upon them the law of love Jesus had said, "Yet a little while I am with you." This declaration called forth Peter's inquiry, "Lord, whither goest Thou?" Then followed the discourse concerning His departure which gathered about the three inquiries of Peter, Thomas, and Philip. In replying to Peter Jesus declared that it was impossible for him to accompany Him, because he was not yet ready, in the most definite and startling words foretelling the fact that Peter would deny Him thrice before the morning broke. He followed this fore-

telling immediately by words full of infinite love, in which He charged the whole
of His disciples not to allow their heart
to be troubled in view of their own un-
readiness for the realisation of their highest
aspirations. The fact that He was leaving
them as to bodily sight would not alter
for one moment His ability to help them.
He reminded them that they believed in
God, Whom they could not see, and
charged them to trust Him also, the inference evidently being, as we have indicated,
that though out of their sight, He would
still be able to help them. He then replied
to Peter's question definitely by telling the
whole of them that He was going to prepare a place for them, that He would come
again and receive them, and that ultimately
they should be with Him. This was a
declaration of His perfect confidence in His
ability to realise their highest aspirations
in spite of all the worst that was in them.
Though Peter could not then follow Him,
because ere the cock should crow he would
thrice deny, yet ultimately He would

follow Him, and be with Him in the Father's house.

At this point Thomas inquired, "How know we the way?" prefacing his question by the declaration, "We know not whither Thou goest." To him the Lord replied, "I am the way, the truth, and the life," and bearing in mind what He had already said, that He was going to the Father, declared that no man could come to the Father but by Him.

The mention of the Father called forth from Philip that great cry of essential humanity, "Show us the Father, and it sufficeth us." It may be that in these words Philip but asked for some epiphany of the Divine glory as Moses had done so long before. Even, however, if this be granted, that desire in itself is evidence of the deep underlying want of humanity, the vision and the knowledge of God. To this cry of Philip Jesus answered first in words which rebuked the slowness of the man who had been so long a time with Him, and yet did not know Him. He then uttered His sublimest claim in simplest words, " He that hath seen Me hath seen the Father." Appealing again to Philip, He declared that both His words and works demonstrated the truth of the claim. Finally, by the use of the solemnly assuring words, "Verily, verily," He declared that the ultimate proofs of the claim would be found in the works which those believing on Him would do, and by the answers to prayer which would be granted to them after His departure to the Father.

ii. Light. The Paraclete

The instruction concerning Light consists of the declaration of Jesus with regard to the coming of the Paraclete; His announcement that this coming would result in a new consciousness of Himself in the experience of the disciples; and in a careful statement concerning the office of the Paraclete.

a. THE COMING OF THE PARACLETE

Though He was leaving them, Another would be given to abide with them. This One He spoke of by the name of Paraclete, and described Him as "the Spirit of truth." In brief words, which are nevertheless conspicuous for their clearness of statement, He declared the method of His coming. The Paraclete comes in answer to the intercession of the Son, from the Father, as His gift. In Himself He is "the Spirit of truth" and the result of His coming, therefore, is inevitably that of light for those to whom He comes. The first value of His presence is that of interpretation and explanation. The things of Christ which had been full of mystery to them would be made clear by the ministry ot the Paraclete. With the disciples He would abide for ever. In this fullness He could not come to the world, for the world would be unable to receive Him, the reason being that the world had not received the Son.

b. THE NEW CONSCIOUSNESS OF CHRIST

The value of the coming of the Paraclete was then declared even more fully as the Lord proceeded to say to His disciples, " I come unto you." Thus the coming of Another was for the making real of the abiding presence of the One Whom they seemed to be losing. The result of His coming would be that of a new union with the Lord Himself, and in that union the three great values of life and light and love would be realised. This is indicated in the actual words of Christ; as to the life union, " Because I live, ye shall live also"; as to the light union, " In that day ye shall know"; as to the love union, "He that hath My commandments, and keepeth them, he it is that loveth Me: and he that loveth Me shall be loved of My Father, and I will love him."

Thus with tender grace the Lord taught these men that His going, which they so much dreaded, really meant His coming to them through the Paraclete in new fashion and new force. Hitherto, He and they, though near to each other, had yet been separated, and they had never fully entered into fellowship with Him. By the coming of the Paraclete they would be united to Him in the force of life and the fullness of light and the fruition of love.

The next interruption to the discourse of Jesus clearly reveals to us the need there was for that new union which would be consummated by the coming of the Paraclete, as it shows how they were unable to understand the teaching of Christ, even though He was present with them.

Judas (not Iscariot), failing to comprehend the meaning of the Master's promise of coming manifestation by the Spirit, asked Him how it was that He would manifest Himself to them and not to the world.

This inquiry must not be lightly passed over. It expressed the supreme difficulty in the minds of the disciples about Jesus. They believed in His Messiahship, but the one thing which they could not understand was that He persisted in hiding this from the world. They would fain have hurried Him to a public manifestation and demonstration of His office, and of Himself; and could not comprehend the reason of this limitation of manifestation.

The answer of the Lord is equally, and supremely of value, showing, as it does, that the limitation was not capricious.

He was perfectly ready to manifest Himself to all those who fulfilled the conditions for receiving the manifestation. These conditions are clearly set forth in the argument of His answer. The power of receptivity is created by obedience. The inspiration of obedience is love. The issue of obedience based upon love is manifestation.

The world had rejected Him, and consequently made impossible its understanding of Him. Full manifestation can only be made progressively. The first gleam of light demands submission and obedience. If that be yielded to, then capacity is created for further revelation. Light had come to men living in darkness. They had disobeyed the light, and so had destroyed their capacity to receive further revelation or manifestation. To those who had been obedient to the measure of light received, it was possible to make further revelation.

c. THE OFFICE OF THE PARACLETE

The Lord next dealt with the office of the Paraclete as to its nature and result.

The nature of the work of the Paraclete is that of the interpretation of the Christ. Sent by the Father in the name of the Son, His mission is that of teaching and bringing to remembrance all that the Son has said.

The first paschal discourse closed with the paragraph which reveals the result of the ministry of the Spirit. Its whole emphasis is suggested by its opening words, " Peace I leave with you." What a strange thing this was for Him to say, and yet by no means strange. Strange, because the story of His going must have been to them the one element which disturbed their peace ; and yet not strange, for the story He had been telling them of the coming of Another was pre-eminently calculated to create peace.

The peace which He bequeathed as a legacy, and which was finally administered by the coming of the Spirit, He differenti-ated from all other peace both as to its quality and its method. Its quality is suggested in the phrase " My peace," which description is interpreted by the words which follow. His peace was that of an untroubled and unfearful heart, even in view of all the terrible suffering and con-flict through which He needs must pass. We are led to inquire what were the secrets of this untroubled and unfearful heart, and three things which He said give us the perfect answer. He saw the issue beyond

the conflict, "I go to the Father." He
was certain of actual victory within the
conflict, "The prince of this world . . .
hath nothing in Me." He was conscious
of the deep purpose of the conflict, "That
the world may know."

Thus bearing the world on His heart in
infinite love, He moved toward the conflict
in which He knew He would be victorious;
toward the ultimate conquest of which He
was certain; and these confidences created
His own sense of peace.

To the disciples He bequeathed this peace,
and they were to enter into possession of
it through the ministry of the Spirit. His
way to the Father He left open, for them
to follow to the ultimate issue; His victory
over the prince of the world He placed at
their disposal, that they also might be
victorious; His love for the world and
message to it He deposited with them,
that it might be published through them.
All these things would become real in
their experience through the advent of the
Paraclete.

iii. LIFE. HIMSELF, PERFECTED IN HIS OWN BY THE SPIRIT

The last movement in the farewell discourses has to do with life. It is, in fact, an elaboration of the teaching concerning the union between Christ and His own, perfected by the Spirit, as to its nature and manifestations. In illustration and illumination it is full of beauty, and if the discrimination may be reverently made, it reaches the highest height and deepest depth in the actual teaching of Christ. All the interruptions of the earlier discourses cease. Only once, still perplexed in the presence of His departure, they inquired among themselves as to His meaning; and once, at the close, expressed their satisfaction at the plainness of His speech.

The discourse is very full, and deals with seven matters. The Lord first illustrated the new union by the figure of the vine; and then proceeded to deal with the relation of the disciples to Himself in this bond of life; their consequent relation to the

world; the office of the Paraclete in relation
to the world; the work of the Paraclete in
the disciples; in order to their equipment
for their work in the world. The discourse
closes with His teaching concerning the
"little while" and its issue; and a summary
as to the meaning of His mission, with a
final word of warning.

a. THE NEW UNION

Under the figure of the vine Jesus explained the new union between Himself
and His people, to be consummated by the
coming of the Spirit. The opening sentence, "I am the true Vine," is inclusive
and exhaustive. It is the seventh "I am"
recorded by John, and, as the Lord's own
exposition will show, it now includes all His
own. They were about to enter into such
relationship with Him that to express the
truth concerning Himself He must needs
include them. His teaching here is certainly almost overwhelming in its revelation
of His grace and power. It is hardly
correct to say that He made the vine the

symbol of relationship. Whereas that would be the truth in some senses, such a statement would miss a deeper principle which is of great value. All earthly things are upon the pattern of heavenly things, and the names of earthly things are borrowed names. Perhaps this may be illustrated by reference to another manifestation of the same principle. Throughout these discourses the Lord spoke much of the Father; and it must ever be remembered that the name " Father," in all the fullness of its meaning, belongs only to God. He has not borrowed an earthly name to teach a heavenly truth. He has rather lent men a heavenly name to indicate to them an earthly responsibility. In this way He is the true Vine. Every vine of earth is an expression of Himself, as are in some sense or degree all created things.

In His use of the figure there are certain words which arrest the attention—" vine," " branches," " fruit." The inter-relation between these is of the closest. Indeed, it is doubtful whether " inter-relation " is not an imperfect word in this connection. The sublime teaching is that of perfect unity. In the presence of the words of Jesus, " I am the Vine," there is no understanding of His meaning save as we take in the whole fact. The vine consists of root and stem and branches and leaves and fruit. The branches are part of the vine; the fruit is also part of the vine, its ultimate issue and intention. How wondrous is this teaching concerning the relationship of His disciples to Him; and how even more wonderful is the fact revealed, that Christ fulfils Himself as to fruit through those who are His own branches! The vine needs the branch for its fruitage; the branch must be part of the vine for the production of fruit.

To take the illustration in the order of statement, He first described the union as in process. "The Father is the husbandman," and His purpose is that of fruit; toward which end He takes away the branches that fail, and cleanses such as are fruitful.

He next insisted upon the conditions for fruitfulness—those of abiding in Him, and of His abiding in the branches.

The blessings following such abiding He declared to be those of prevailing prayer and abounding fruitfulness.

Finally, He revealed the pattern of the union. He first declared His Father's love for Him, and then that His love for them was of the same nature. Having thus revealed the eternal depths of love, and the channel of that love toward them, He commanded them to abide therein. Not, let it be most carefully noted, to abide in their love to Him, but in His love to them— that love being at once the atmosphere of their love, the impulse of their activity, and the strength of their service. Having thus argued that the love of the Father was their place of safety, and so revealed a privilege, He laid upon them the consequent responsibility, and emphasised it by an argument back to the Father. The way for them to abide in His love was to keep His commandments, and the pattern of their obedience to His commandments was that of His obedience to His Father's commandments, through which obedience He abode in His Father's love.

b. THE DISCIPLES AND THE CHRIST

The Lord immediately proceeded to describe in yet fuller detail the experimental relation between His disciples and Himself. He had spoken these words to them in order that His joy might be in them, and that so their joy might be fulfilled. His joy was that of doing the will of His Father in answer to the love of His Father. So great was this joy that He desired that they also might share it by delighting in His will in answer to His love for them.

Then He declared the whole of such experience to be that of love, and He laid upon them His great commandment that they love one another, and taught them that their love for each other must be upon the pattern of His love for them. To enter into His joy they must abide in His love, and that love for Him must be manifested by their love one for another.

He then declared the fullness of the relation between Himself and them in the new economy, by using the great word "friends," affirming that He gave them the supreme proof of friendship in revealing to them His deepest secrets, namely all the things which He had heard from His Father.

All this was in order that they might be admitted to the sphere in which they might fulfil the purposes already dealt with, those of abounding fruitfulness, and prevailing prayer.

c. THE DISCIPLES AND THE WORLD

While all this teaching was intended for His own, its ultimate issue was that of blessing to the world; and He proceeded to show them what the perfecting of His life in them would mean, as to the relation between the disciples and the world.

Again He charged them, in view of what He was about to teach them, that the one law of their life must be that of love one toward another. The life of relationship to Him, issuing in likeness to Him, would necessarily bring upon them the hatred and persecution of the world, as it had already brought it upon Him. He showed them that they could expect no other, and in this connection the same sequence of relationship was in His mind. The world would hate them because they would reveal Him, and it had already hated Him. The awful meaning of this hatred He declared to be hatred of the Father. The world's hatred of Christ was due to the world's wandering from God, and ignorance of God. The life and teaching of Jesus, revealing the Father, rebuked and contradicted this degraded life, which was out of harmony with the Divine will. The measure in which His disciples would produce the fruitage of His life would be the measure of their revelation of the Father, and consequently of their protest against worldliness, and therefore also, the measure of the world's hatred of them. To share

His life must be to have fellowship in His suffering.

Yet the Lord saw the larger possibility of blessing for the world, and He told them that when the Paraclete was come, He, together with them, would bear witness. Thus the testimony which the world needed and would receive, would be that of witness to the One Whom it had rejected, and so to truth concerning God. In the new economy that testimony would be borne by the Paraclete in co-operation with the Church.

d. THE WORLD AND THE PARACLETE

The carefulness of the Lord to prepare His disciples for all He saw coming to them is remarkably revealed in this section. He declared that He had spoken in order that they should not be made to stumble, and then proceeded to give them a yet more detailed account of the persecution to which they would be subjected. That persecution would result from the world's darkness. It would be so violent that the time would come when those who killed them would think that they did God service. In that He revealed the reason for the violence of the opposition which they might expect. No bitterness is so dreadful as that which is based upon a religious conviction, even though it be fanatical.

An almost startling picture is presented of the great tenderness and patience of the Master. He was perfectly conscious of the imperfection of their understanding, and yet in searching words He gently rebuked them because their sorrow, that is the sorrow of which He was conscious as He spoke to them, was really sorrow on account of their own suffering. So little were they occupied with Him, that they were not even anxious to know where He was going. In spite of all this He continued to teach them with great patience, declaring to them many things that they did not then understand, storing their memories with gracious words, the values of which they would gather in the day of the Spirit's illumination. In view of the

206

persecution that awaited them, and the
work committed to them, they needed the
perfect equipment of the coming of the
Paraclete, and He could not come save as
Jesus departed. Here, as everywhere, the
painful process had an underlying reason
of infinite wisdom and tender love.

The world was still in the mind of
the Master, and its seeking and salvation
created the burden which lay constantly
on His heart. Therefore before detailing
the facts of the Spirit's work in the believer,
He spoke of the larger value of that work
for the world. In a few brief sentences
He gave a perfect statement of the facts
of the mission of the Holy Spirit in the
world. The method of the Spirit in that
application is revealed in one word, "convict."
He would so present the truth as to carry
conviction. How the world would respond
to the truth is another matter, not now
dealt with. The office of the Spirit is to
convict, and the truth is always centred
in Christ. The subjects concerning which
He brings conviction to the soul of man

are seen as related to, and affected by, the Person and work of Jesus. These subjects are those of sin, of righteousness, and of judgment; and in each case the Lord distinctly stated the relation His work bears to these subjects, and made a deduction of importance.

With regard to sin, the Spirit's conviction establishes the claim of Jesus to be able to save from sin, and declares the nature of sin therefore to be that of refusal to believe in Him.

With regard to righteousness, the Spirit declares the realisation of it in the life of Jesus, by stating the fact that He has gone to the Father, and thus implies the possibility which He creates of others living the life of righteousness.

With reference to judgment, the Spirit convinces of a victory already gained, and a judgment pronounced by Christ over the prince of the world. Such fact of victory at once suggests a possibility of freedom from the dominion of the evil one, and utters a warning that those who refuse to share in the victory won, must participate in the judgment pronounced.

This section should be read in the light of the statement made in an earlier declaration, " He shall bear witness of Me : and ye also bear witness." This is the whole Gospel, and is to be testified to the world by the Spirit through believers.

e. THE DISCIPLES AND THE PARACLETE

The Lord then declared how the Spirit would first testify to the disciples themselves in order to the bearing of this witness to the world. The great principles of revelation are clearly set forth. He first declared His own knowledge in words which must not be hurried over, even though they only constitute part of a sentence, " I have many things to say." The disciples of Jesus must ever remember that there are no mysteries to Him. The things which we cannot understand are clear to Him as the light of day. Then it is also true, and never to be forgotten, that He has these things to say to His disciples. He does not arbitrarily withhold knowledge, for all He knows is at the disposal of His own, and His will is that they should know perfectly the things of God. It is, however, impossible for Him to communicate to them, save as they are able to bear. He therefore adapts His teaching to their capacity. The stupendous nature of truth is such that it would hopelessly crush men if revealed to them save as they are prepared for its reception. An illustration of this is to be found in His apparent slowness to tell them of His Cross ; and moreover, that in the fact that when He did declare it, He never unfolded all its meaning. For the unfolding of this, and of all truth concerning Himself, they had to wait the preparation to receive, which would come to them with the coming of the Paraclete, Who would guide them into the truth. The force of this expression should be carefully noted. Not that He would teach them truth, but that He would guide them into it. This is far more than the impartation of truth to the intellect. It is the bringing of life into a realm conditioned within truth. In this is laid bare the law of progression. An intellectual apprehension of truth demands response in character and conduct, and it is by this response that the disciple is prepared for the reception of fuller unfoldings of truth.

Here also, the truth has its definition and its purpose. The purpose is that of glorifying Christ, and its definition is the perfect knowledge of Christ. The whole statement of this important teaching may thus be summarised. The things of the Father have been focussed for us in the Son, and are revealed to us by the Spirit as He interprets to us the meaning of the Son. This revelation proceeds according to our capacity. Our capacity is enlarged in proportion as we are obedient to the truth, and sanctified by it.

f. THE " LITTLE WHILE "

The fact of their inability to bear the truth was at once manifested by their evident perplexity at what He had said. They did not know, they could not understand what He meant by the " little while," or by His statement that He was going to the Father. He therefore patiently explained to them that the "little while" of their sorrow would be caused by His going, and by His consequent absence from them. Very tender was His recognition of the natural sorrow which would fill their hearts on account of His going. He knew that they could not yet follow Him, and would not be able to understand the mystery of His dying; and immediately spoke to them of the coming joy which would result from the presence of the Paraclete, Who would bring Him back to them, and by Whose coming therefore, they would see Him more perfectly than ever before. He knew, and told them, that by His coming a new joy would enter into their lives, and proceeded to teach them how wonderful a life they would enter upon in the new fellowship with Himself which would result.

The wonder of this life He revealed as being twofold. First there would be no need to ask Him questions, for the Spirit would guide them into truth; and consequently they would be able to ask the Father, and whatever they asked in the name of the Son would be granted.[1]

Thus the double value of the Spirit's coming is revealed as the passing of perplexity, resulting from the Spirit's interpretation; and the life of prevailing prayer which will be based upon the Spirit's revelation of the Christ, which inspires prayer within the sphere of His name, and so ensures the answer of the Father.

g. THE SUMMARY OF TEACHING

This is the closing section of the paschal discourses. The Lord now distinctly told His disciples that He had been speaking

---

[1] It must be carefully noted that the word "ask" in verse nineteen, and in the first part of verse twenty-three, is an entirely different word from the word "ask" in the latter part of verse twenty-three and in verse twenty-four. The former word refers to the asking of questions, and the second to prayer.

to them in proverbs, but that an hour was approaching in which He would speak no more in proverbs, but tell them plainly of the Father.

There can be no doubt that this was again a reference to the coming of the Paraclete, for He proceeded to declare that in that day they would be able to ask [1] the Father, and the Father would answer them for the love He bears them.

The last actual words of the discourse constitute a sublime and majestic declaration concerning Himself. In all probability He had never said anything quite like this to them. He spoke as the Son of God in the sphere of His own eternity, first declaring the incomprehensible fact, " I came out from the Father"; and secondly, the manifestation of that fact, " and am come into the world." He then announced His self-determined purpose of leaving the world, " I leave the world"; and finally, declared His destination, "and go unto the Father."

[1] Here the word refers to prayer and not inquiry.

Thus in briefest space and simplest words we have a declaration of the whole redemptive progress of the Son of God. From the Father into the world; in the world manifesting the Father; from the world unto the Father.

The disciples immediately asserted their understanding of such a statement. Said they, "Lo, now speakest Thou plainly, and speakest no proverb." They announced moreover, their belief that He indeed came forth from God.

With gentle pity He showed them that while they might be convinced of the fact, they had little understanding of its nature, telling them that the hour had positively come in which they would desert Him; and yet in view of that desertion He spoke to them the word of peace, and bade them be of good cheer, because He had overcome the world.

216

iv. THE PRAYER OF THE WORD

The final section of the division dealing with the Manifestation to His own, records for us the Prayer of the Word. Let our meditation of it, marvellous and comprehensive as it is, be reverent, and with abiding sense of our inability perfectly to comprehend.

As in the discourses, so here, the line of thought is that of an unveiling of life, of light, and of love. The fact of life is revealed in the words in which the Word spoke of His relation to His Father, and uttered His petition for Himself. The fact of light is manifested in the things He said of His relation to the men by whom He was surrounded, and in the petitions He uttered for them. The fact of love is supremely evident in His prayer for the Church, as He sought its unity and perfecting.

a. LIFE. THE WORD AND THE FATHER

The first movement of the prayer was wholly within the realm of the relation of the Son to His Father, and of that work through which new relationship between man and God was made possible. The petition was that the Father would glorify the Son, and its reason was that the Son might glorify the Father. Thus again, under the shadow of the Cross though the petition was for something to be granted to Himself, it was characterised by absolute unselfishness, and afforded a new and splendid manifestation of the fact that devotion to the will of His Father was the one passion of His life.

This petition for the glorification of the Son is explained in the words which follow. "As Thou gavest Him authority over all flesh, that whatsoever Thou hast given Him, to them He should give eternal life." As we read these words our minds revert immediately to the tenth chapter of the Gospel, in which we have the record of His declaration that He would lay down His life, and take it again, having received authority to do this from His Father. He now prayed that the Son might be glorified in carrying

218

out that programme, so that men should come to the knowledge of God, and the Father thus be glorified.

This petition therefore for the glorification of the Son moved in perfect harmony with the Divine will, and asked for the Cross.

The plea urged was that of the victory already won, " I glorified Thee on the earth."

This part of the prayer ended with a repetition of the request that the Son might be glorified in fellowship with the Father. The Word asked that the Father would carry out all the intention of His will for the laying down of the life of the Son, and the taking of it again for impartation to men. Never was there such a shining revelation of the true realm of prayer.

b. LIGHT. THE WORD AND THE MEN

The prayer now passed into petitions which were wholly concerned with the men who were immediately associated with Him at the time of its offering. Out of the midst of those rejecting Him, a few had

been obedient to the heavenly light, and
had yielded themselves to Him as Lord
and Master. To this little circle He had
given the words which His Father had given
Him, and thus manifested to them the
name of His Father. It is interesting to
notice the confidence that Christ had in
these men. He did not say that they
understood the things He had spoken to
them. He did say that they *knew* that
what He had spoken had been received
from Him by God, and that He Himself had
come from God. Their faith was centred
in Him as a Person, and in the fact that
He was the authorised and sent Messenger
of the covenant. So far His work had been
successful. In them He declared He was
glorified, and now He prayed not for the
world, but for them.

We must not however for one moment
imagine that Christ had abandoned the
world, or ceased to care for it. On the
contrary, His interest in the disciples was
a proof of His larger interest in all those
who had refused Him. He knew that this

group of men, in whom He by the Spirit
would dwell, would carry on His enter-
prises, and through their witness those in
darkness would yet be brought into the
light. His prayer for them therefore was
not one of indifference to the need of the
world, but rather one born of abiding love
for the world, which sought the perfecting
of the instruments through which He might
reach the world.

For these men He asked two things, one
having to do with their life, and the other
with their service. In the presence of His
Father He spoke of their coming loneliness.
There was a touch of ineffable tenderness
in the words in which He contrasted them
with Himself. While He was about to
leave the world and to go to the Father,
these were still to be in the midst of the
forces which had rejected and were about
to crucify Him. He prayed that they
might be kept. In asking this He spoke
to God as "Holy Father," a remarkably
suggestive title in this connection. More
than anything else, these men would need

holiness of character for the witness they were to bear, and for the suffering they were to share they would need tender and loving care. He recognised that all their need must be supplied from the One Who had sent Him to them, and to Whom He was now returning, and in this method of address there was a suggestion of His confidence in His Father's perfect ability to meet that need. He asked that the men who would need holiness might be kept by the One Who is holy. He asked that the men who would need tender, loving care, might be kept by the One Who is essentially Father.

The unsullied light of the Divine holiness He knew, and knew moreover, the infinite strength that is ever supplied to those who walk in the light. He knew the unfathomable deeps of the love of the heart of His eternal Father, and knew moreover, the absolute safety of such as are kept in that love.

How often during the days preceding this prayer had He known the force of temptation, and proved the absolute safety of life responsive to the claim of the Holy God. How often had men assailed Him, attempting to arrest and harm Him, and were unable until His hour had come, because He was kept by the infinite and unsearchable love of God.

He knew the position these men would occupy after He had left them. Their relation to Him had already produced hatred of them on the part of those who hated Him. What that would mean in the coming days He knew right well, and yet He did not pray that they should be taken out of the world, and this for two reasons. First for their own sakes, for He knew the value of the testing, and the buffeting, that they must also be perfected through suffering. Secondly for the world's sake. Twice He said, "They are not of the world, even as I am not of the world." This statement must be understood as revealing not merely His separation from the world, but His identification with it. He was not of the world as to its conception and manner of life. He was of the world as to identification with it for its uplifting and salvation. It is not sufficient barely to affirm that the disciple is not of the world. The statement must always be qualified by the words of Jesus, "*Even as I am not.*" These men would not now belong to the world in its degradation, but they would belong to it for its salvation.

This is even more clearly indicated in the words, "As Thou didst send Me into the world, even so send I them into the world." He had been sent to reveal the Father, to seek and to save the lost. They were to be sent for exactly the same purpose. He had sanctified Himself, that is, set Himself apart to the mission for which the Father had sent Him; and the reason of His sanctification was that they might be sanctified, that is, set apart to the fulfilment of His mission in the world. Power to save ever lies in separation. The true ideal of sanctification is separation from all that is unlike and contrary to God, so that in identification there may be the communication of the power of God which uplifts.

c. LOVE. THE WORD AND THE CHURCH

In all this wonderful prayer there is no sentence more full of comfort for us than this, " Neither for these only do I pray, but for them also that believe on Me through their word." In this last movement the Lord looked beyond the men immediately surrounding Him, through the vista of the coming centuries, and saw in one comprehensive glance all that the Father had given Him, who would be gathered to Him through the message and the ministry of those for whom He had been praying; and seeing all, He prayed for all. Every disciple of Christ may find a place in this great intercessory prayer, being able to say, He saw me, He prayed for me.

His first desire for His own was one having application to their ministry in the world. He asked that " they all may be one " in God and in Himself; one that is,

first with Him and the Father, and therefore
one with each other. Here again it is
clearly seen that the ultimate purpose was
the blessing of the world. He prayed for
the unity of His own, "that the world may
believe that thou didst send Me." By the
manifestation of the vital communion between the Church and God in Christ the
world is to have its opportunity of belief
in Him.

In order to this unity the Lord declared
that He had placed at the disposal of His
people the glory which God had given Him.
What that glory is, must be gathered
from former statements and considerations.
In His case it was the commandment,
authority, or right to lay down His life, and
take it again for the blessing of others. Is
not therefore the supreme glory that Christ
has bestowed upon the Church the right
to suffer with Him in the salvation and
uplifting of men? It is by this glory that
men are to know that Christ was the Sent
of the Father. What a sacred and wonderful deposit this is. Wherever the Church

has realised it, and manifested it, her testimony has been victorious.

The closing words of the intercessory prayer reveal the final purpose of the Lord for His Church. This He expressed to His Father not in the form of a request, but rather as the declaration of a settled purpose. Thus the prayer reached its climax in the revelation of His attitude of perfect and peculiar fellowship with God. He Who had accomplished the will of God, and Who through His coming baptism was confident of final accomplishment, declared His will for His people, knowing that here also His will was in perfect harmony with that of His Father.

How wonderful a declaration, and how marvellous a manifestation of love to the Church, these words afford. His will for His own was, first that they might be with Him ; and secondly that they might observe His glory. Of these the first is in itself sufficient to fill the heart with joy unutterable. To be with Him is to realise all highest aspirations ; and for occupation what can be greater than the observing of His glory? So far we have but seen that glory dimly, as in a mirror, and at a distance. At last in perfect light and closest fellowship we shall learn the unsearchable riches of the Son, and therefore of the Father also.

230

III. BY THE CROSS

We now come to the final movement in the great mission of manifestation. We approach the infinite and superlative mystery. Yet here mystery becomes revelation. Here it behoves us while desiring to look into these things, to do so in the attitude of hushed and adoring wonder, knowing that there are deeps of light beyond the possibility of our seeing. It is well that we should attempt to keep our attention fixed on the central Person. Others will cross and recross the scene, but they are all subsidiary, and only to be glanced at in order that the understanding of the One may be more complete. In the manifestation by the Cross those essential and eternal facts which have occupied our attention in all the earlier movements are still present. The first revelation is that of Love, deserted, and yet faithful. The second is that of Light, eclipsed, and breaking forth into new radiance. The last is that of Life, laid down, and thus given to others.

i. Love, Deserted and Faithful

Love, deserted, and yet faithful, is revealed in the garden, and the two trial scenes.

a. THE GARDEN

From the sacred hours of teaching and prayer the Lord passed immediately to the final acts in His mighty work. Crossing the Kidron, He entered Gethsemane in the company of His disciples. It was evidently a familiar spot. John distinctly declares that "Jesus oft-times resorted thither with His disciples." This familiarity with the haunts of the Lord served the traitor now, and thither he led the band of men who were commissioned to arrest Jesus.

Here, in the hour of His weakness, He revealed the voluntary nature of that weakness in such a way as for one brief moment to halt His foes in helpless suspense before Him, some of whom, utterly paralysed, fell to the ground. These men had come to seek Him, and, suddenly presenting himself before them, He asked whom they sought.

When they told Him, He said, "I am." At that moment "they went backward, and fell to the ground." It is perfectly evident that with the uttering of that word He flashed upon the men who were approaching Him some evidence of His power and majesty. It was not merely in the formula, "I am," which might have made its appeal to Hebrews, but which would have no significance to Gentiles, but in some other way He made these men conscious for a passing moment of His majesty. Yet immediately whatever appearance of glory astonished them was veiled, and in meekness He yielded Himself to them, and with tender consideration for His disciples asked that they might not be arrested, but permitted to go their way.

How paltry Peter's use of the sword appears, in view of such marvellous restraint. In this scene the most wonderful facts flame out upon our astonished vision. The majesty and the meekness of our Lord are alike revealed, and we hardly know at which we wonder most.

b. THE TRIALS

1. *Before the Priests*

The meekness of the Word fills us with astonishment as we watch Him, allowing Himself to be seized, and bound, and led away. It is beyond the power of human love to understand how, while so able to defend Himself and destroy all His enemies, He yet submitted to the seizing, and the binding, and the leading. There can be no explanation of it save that afforded in the words :

Love divine, all loves excelling.

Equally amazing is the fact that men who, but a moment before, in the presence of some surprising manifestation, should have fallen to the earth with fear, now dared to lay hands on Him with murderous intent. Surely here, as through all the story, there is evidenced the awfulness of sin, and the unfathomable love of the Divine heart.

From the garden the Lord was taken to the court of the high priests. There was absolutely no civil charge that could be urged against Him ; but before His death could be encompassed, such a charge must be formulated. With this end in view, He was arraigned ; and in all the annals of human crime there is nothing more utterly degraded and despicable than this attempt on the part of the priests to entangle an innocent man by cross-examination, in order that they might find in His own words some ground upon which they might encompass His death. Submitting Himself as He did to death, He yet sternly rebuked the wickedness of the method employed by these, His chief enemies. Thus, while He was prepared in infinite love to bear the sin of the world, out of the midst of His sorrows He made no truce w.th sin, but sternly rebuked it.

How sad a picture is that of Peter in these hours of his Lord's suffering. Introduced to the house of the high priests by John, he allowed himself to be driven by the saucy sarcasm of a servant-maid into open denial. The details of the story afford a solemn warning as to the triviality of the things over which men of splendid capacity may fall to terrible depths.

2. *Before Pilate*

Jesus was now sent to the palace of Pilate the governor, and John records a fact concerning the priests which is very suggestive. These men who, by methods most dishonest, had formulated a charge against Him, yet would not enter into the Roman palace lest they should be defiled. What a startling revelation this is of the degradation of the religious idea as represented by these men. Stooping to all meanness and baseness to encompass the death of One against Whom no evil could be affirmed, they were yet punctilious in their observance of the traditions of cleanness.

The scene at the private interview between Pilate and Jesus would form a subject full of possibility for the brush of an artist. The representative of Roman power was confronted with a Man of the people, Who yet had about Him an inscrutable air of Kingliness. When the

Roman asked Him what it was that He
had done to arouse the hatred of the priests,
His reply was such as must have sounded
strange in the ears of Pilate. He spoke
three times of "My Kingdom," declaring
that essentially it was not of this world,
and therefore could not be established by
worldly methods.

The procurator, recognising the inferential
claim, asked Him in surprise, "Art Thou
a King then?" In reply the Lord not
only claimed Kingship, but revealed the
nature of His Kingdom, claiming to be
King over the whole realm of truth.
Pilate's question, "What is truth?" was in
all probability one of satirical scorn, not so
much for the Man before him, as for
His evident ideals. His after-attempts to
save Him proved that in his heart there
was both respect and pity for Jesus; but
he had lived so long in the hard unreality
of things, and had seen so much of the
world's deceit, that he had ceased to believe
in the power of truth, and hence his
question.

From that conversation the governor went to face the Jews, with evident determination to save Jesus from them. This he did by reminding them of his custom to release a prisoner unto them, and offering them Barabbas, a robber, as an alternative to Jesus. The sequel proved how little even Pilate knew of the lengths to which a degraded priesthood would go to encompass its purpose, born of hatred. Instructed by the priests, the assembled crowd clamoured for Barabbas.

The governor, defeated in his first attempt, now adopted a new method. It was a terrible one, consisting of the scourging, and crowning, and buffeting of Jesus. All this took place within the palace, according to Roman law, and in all probability out of sight of the rabble. This being accomplished, Pilate went out and announced to the crowd that he would bring Jesus forth, seeing that even after scourging he found no fault in Him. Following the announcement, Jesus came forth, " wearing a crown of thorns and the purple garment." Pilate's introduction of Him, all bleeding from the Roman rods, was significant, "Behold, the Man!" It is almost impossible thus to follow the details without believing that Pilate hoped to stir them to pity by the awful sight. Again it is evident that he did not know the capacity of the human heart for hatred, for the sight that should have stirred their pity but served to call forth their lust for revenge, which expressed itself in one repeated word, "Crucify!" "Crucify!" With infinite scorn the Roman said, "Take Him yourselves, and crucify Him; for I find no crime in Him." To this they replied that the supreme reason for His death was that He had claimed to be the Son of God.

Through all this the most impressive fact is that of the silence of Jesus. It was the silence of infinite and overwhelming love. The crown of thorns, the purple of mockery, and the buffeting of brutality, drew forth from Him no word either of complaint or of rebuke.

The latest charge of the Jews that He had claimed to be the Son of God filled Pilate with a new fear. Was it possible that this strange Man Who had spoken of a Kingdom of truth, over which He presided, was indeed Divine? He took Him again into the palace, away from the mob, and questioned Him. He spoke to Him of his authority to release or crucify Him, to which Jesus replied that his authority was not supreme but delegated, and charged the priests with the greater sin, in that they had delivered Him to Pilate.

If His silence was the silence of love, so also was His speech the speech of love. In it He interpreted the reason of His silence. He recognised that through all this process He was still co-operating with God in the infinite purposes of His love.

Coming forth from the interview, Pilate once again sought to release Him, but now the priests used the final argument with such a man as Pilate. They suggested that to free this Man would prove his disloyalty to Cæsar.

Bringing the Prisoner forth—and what an awful vision of suffering He must have presented—he said to them with evident sarcasm, " Behold, your King ! " They clamoured for His death, and still mocking them, he inquired, " Shall I crucify your King ? " The intensity of their hatred for Jesus is evidenced in their answer, " We have no king but Cæsar." They hated the rule of the Cæsars, and would have done anything to have broken the yoke of their bondage, and yet they bowed to that yoke, and hugged that chain, in order to encompass the casting out of the One Whose life and teaching had rebuked them.

That last word was an unanswerable argument for Pilate. The conscience must be disobeyed in order to retain the favour of Cæsar, and the consequent comforts of life. Thus the governor refused the King of truth for fear of offending Cæsar, and ere long Cæsar cast him off. Thus the priests led the nation in a new submission to Cæsar for the casting out of

Christ, and at last Cæsar ground the nation to powder beneath his iron heel.

ii. LIGHT, ECLIPSED AND DAWNING

a. THE CRUCIFIXION

In sublimity and simplicity John chronicles the most stupendous fact in human history, a fact at once terrible as an outworking of sin, and transcendent as an accomplishment of love, " *They crucified Him.*"

There is no detailed description, and the only fitting attitude of the spirit is that of the subdued awe which, while conscious of the terrible scene, yet shuts it out from all curious contemplation. Standing before that Cross one can but tremble at sin, and wonder at Love. There between the thieves is the Crowned Sorrow, crowned as to its measure, for never such was seen before or since ; crowned also in its value, for the cup there drained to the dregs will for evermore overflow with the elixir of a new life for a death-doomed race.

How little those who stood around under-

stood the meaning of that hour. They had
cast Him from the Temple, the City, and
the Nation. Outside the Temple, He
destroyed it. Outside the City, He sealed
its doom. Outside the Nation, He scattered
it, and made it for long ages a hissing and a
byeword in the earth. And yet in co-
operation with God He laid the foundation
of the new and spiritual Temple, initiated
the building of the City that hath the
foundations, and liberated the life through
which should come the generation of the
new Nation. Was ever the folly, the
wickedness, the sin of man so evident?
Was ever the wisdom, the power, the love
of God so demonstrated?

Over the Cross Pilate caused to be affixed
the title, "JESUS OF NAZARETH, THE KING
OF THE JEWS." The priests, offended at the
inscription, endeavoured to persuade him to
change it. He had however yielded to them
already, to the hurt of his own conscience,
and now doggedly declined to make any
change. All unconsciously, and in more
senses than one, how prophetic was that

description. In His weakness and out-
casting He was indeed a picture of the King
of the Jews. They who gave Him such a
throne were to become such a nation as, on
the side of its degradation, the Cross suggested. And yet changing their rejection
into actual coronation by the working of
His mighty love, He became the one and
only King of Whose Kingdom there should
be no end. Out of the abysmal darkness
flamed the essential Light of the eternities.

b. THE ONLOOKERS

How vulgar is the picture of the soldiers,
as in the presence of the dying Sufferer
they indulged in commonplace gambling for
His garments. Yet viewed from the higher
standpoint, even they in brutal ignorance
fulfilled ancient prophecies, and co-operated
in the working of Divine purposes.

One sad and sorrowful group of women
stood near the Cross; at its centre His
Mother, bereaved and broken hearted. Yet
again even the sword-pierced soul of the
Virgin occasioned a radiant manifestation

of His tenderness. He provided for what remained to her of sorrow-shadowed life, by committing her to the care of the disciple whom He had so dearly loved.

C. THE ACCOMPLISHMENT

Not until all things were accomplished did any word escape Him as to His human agony. Then all the pent-up suffering of the awful hours found vent in one brief and fearful cry, " I thirst." When they had offered Him the potion which would have deadened His consciousness on the occasion when His spiritual anguish found expression in words chronicled by Matthew and Mark, He had refused it. But now that they offered Him vinegar after the cry which revealed His physical agony, He received it and uttered the words which spoke of the mightiest of all victories, " It is finished." All was accomplished that would give such value to His death as should be available for the redemption of man. Nothing now remained but that there should be the outward and physical expression of that spiritual death through which He had passed. To that outward expression He passed of His own majestic will, "He gave up the ghost." This statement is in perfect harmony with, and carries out into actual accomplishment what He had Himself declared, that no man should take His life, but that He would lay it down of Himself.

iii. LIFE, LAID DOWN AND GIVEN

a. THE ENEMIES

Attempts have been made to prove that the flowing forth of blood and water from the side of the Saviour, when pierced by the soldier, was a natural sequence of the manner of His death. All such attempts are without foundation. The only hypothesis upon which the argument is based includes the necessity for denying the statement of Scripture that the Holy One of God did not see corruption. The process described by those who hold that the separation of blood from water was natural is in itself the first stage of corruption. There is no doubt that this flowing forth was a mystery not to be accounted for by natural laws. The fact that it was a mystery caused John to make his careful statement, that he himself saw and gave testimony to what otherwise would be incredible, but which was significant and symbolic and a part of that mystery in which the Person and mission of Jesus are for ever shrouded.

To take the words blood and water, and carefully to trace them through the writings of John, marking well his use of them, is to discover the significance of this remarkable fact. Blood is always the symbol of the natural life, and water of the spiritual. The outflowing of the blood was the symbol of that marvel by which the vice of the natural man is cleansed ; and the outflowing of the water was the symbol of that great result by which virtue is made possible to men in the power of life communicated by the Spirit of God. The blood speaks of redemption, and the water of regeneration.

b. THE LOVERS

Tender and beautiful indeed is the picture of the two secret disciples coming to the attitude of a great courage, and expressing that courage in their fulfilment of the last tender offices of respect to the body of their Lord. Joseph found Him a grave in his garden, and Nicodemus brought great wealth of spices for His entombment.

C. TO EVERLASTING. xx., xxi.

I. ABIDING LIFE. xx. 1-18

i. THE TOMB EMPTY. 1-10
a. Mary. The Stone taken away.
b. John. The linen Cloths lying.
c. Peter. The linen Cloths lying, and the Napkin.

ii. THE LORD ALIVE. 11-18
a. Mary alone.
b. Mary and the Angels.
c. Mary and Jesus.
d. Mary and the Disciples.

II. ABIDING LIGHT. xx. 19-31

i. THE DISCIPLES. 19-23
a. The Assembly in fear.
b. Jesus in the midst. Peace pronounced.
c. The prophetic Breathing. Peace promised.

ii. THOMAS. 24-29
a. The Difficulty. 24, 25
b. The Illumination. 26-29

iii. UNRECORDED SIGNS. 30, 31

III. ABIDING LOVE. xxi.

i. BREAKFAST. 1-14
a. The fruitless Night. 1-3
b. The morning Vision. 4-8
c. The Meal. 9-14

ii. LOVE TRIUMPHANT. 15-23
a. The threefold Challenge.
b. The threefold Confession.
c. The threefold Commission.

iii. UNRECORDED DEEDS. 24, 25

250

C. TO EVERLASTING

The last division of the Gospel is brief but full of suggestion and value. As the first division declared the way by which the Word came from ages past into manifestation in Time; this reveals the abiding conditions of the Word toward His own in all ages to come. The abiding Life is demonstrated by the empty tomb and the living Lord. The abiding Light is seen in His appearances to His disciples, and His patience with Thomas. The abiding Love is manifested in His interest in the material needs of His disciples, and in the tenderness of His dealing with the spiritual need of Peter.

I. ABIDING LIFE

i. THE TOMB EMPTY

This is the story of a dark morning and a lost Master. It gathers around three of His disciples, Mary of Magdala, John, and Peter. Their condition was that of sadness and perplexity in the presence

251

of a loss which had become enshrouded in a new mystery. That mystery was caused by the fact that the stone was rolled away from the mouth of the tomb, and the tomb itself was empty. The grave-cloths were lying there, strangely undisturbed, but the loved One which they had enshrouded was absent.

What excitement all this produced is evidenced by the fact that the three disciples mentioned are all of them described as running. Mary ran to tell the disciples, and John and Peter ran to the grave. The words of Mary most graphically reveal the troubled state of heart in which they found themselves. "They have taken away the Lord out of the tomb, and we know not where they have laid Him." So strange and perplexing was it that Peter and John "went away again unto their own home."

Before doing so however, notwithstanding the fact that their perplexity had been deepened, a new conviction had taken possession of them. At the first John saw "the linen cloths lying," yet reverently remained outside. Peter entered, and the word which described his examination, "he *beholdeth* the linen cloths lying," is a stronger one, and suggests careful scrutiny. Following him, John entered, and what he saw resulted in belief. The strange and inexplicable vision upon which their eyes rested was that of the carefully folded grave-cloths, remaining as they had been bound about the body of Jesus, not folded together as garments that had been unwrapped, but still in the folds which had encompassed His body. Yet, even though there came to John the conviction that the Lord was alive, there was no personal demonstration of the fact. They had not seen the Lord Himself. That hour of darkness preceding the dawn, with all its rapid movement of excitement, and strange emotion of mystery, and apparent aimlessness of action, was symbolic of what Christianity would have been apart from the living Christ. Hopes disappointed, and renewed without assurance; love bereft, and hoping without possession; faith vanquished, and inquiring without certainty.

ii. THE LORD ALIVE

Mary did not follow the disciples to their home. She lingered still, even though she had lost her Lord. The sad, disconsolate woman, in the dull grey of the morning, was a type of deepest sorrow. Such tears as hers, the tears of deepest love, have often clarified the vision; and as presently she stooped once more to look into the darkness of the empty grave she saw a vision of angels. It would seem as though her grief were now too great for her to be startled by anything, for when the angels asked her, "Woman, why weepest thou?" she told them the same story of her lost Lord; and so great was her emotion that she did not stay to gaze upon the wonderful angels. Even their dazzling splendour did not fill the gap in her heart. She turned from them because He was not there, to look out again at the garden.

Having done so, she saw One Who

asked her the same question which the angels had asked. In answering the Stranger, the strength of her love flamed forth as she said if only He would tell her what He had done with her Lord, she would take Him away. How little love thinks of labour !

It was then He spoke, using the old, familiar name, " Mary." In a moment she responded, " Rabboni," as the agony passed from her spirit in the consciousness of His living presence.

Her cry was that of deep love, and yet of imperfect understanding. It suggested that now the old relationship would be restored, that once again she possessed Him as a Master, Who would be with her in bodily form to direct, control, suggest. It was this mistaken thought that Jesus corrected when He forbade her touching Him until, having ascended, she could enter upon a new relationship with Him which as yet she did not understand. He would no longer be to her One Who could be missed because He could be touched; but henceforth an ever-present One to spiritual consciousness, because not present to the consciousness which was material only.

Having thus corrected her, He made her the first living witness of His resurrection by sending her to the disciples, whom He tenderly and beautifully described as " My brethren."

In this picture that which supremely impresses us is the fact that the risen Lord was changed, so that, save at His own will, He was unknown to those who had known Him in the past; and yet was so actually the same that when He, either by word or touch revealed Himself, there was no questioning His identity.

II. ABIDING LIGHT

i. The Disciples

On that memorable resurrection-day John records the morning and evening appearances. Between the interview with Mary in the morning and His meeting with His disciples in the evening, He had in all probability seen Peter alone, and journeyed with the two men to Emmaus. His coming into the evening assembly was so remarkable, that it must have been an experience never to be forgotten by those who were present. The fact that they were all together was due to the happenings of the morning. They were regathered by a mystery. The empty grave, the undisturbed grave-cloths, the testimony of Mary, all combined to declare that the One Whom they had seen crucified was alive. Yet the dominant mental attitude was that of fear. They were gathered in secret, and within closed doors.

Suddenly, without the opening of the doors, the Lord stood in their midst, and greeted them with the ordinary salutation of the day, " Peace unto you." This salutation was filled with a new meaning as He accompanied it by showing them His hands and His side. It was His answer to their fear, and was intended to demonstrate the fact of His resurrection and leave no room for doubt that He was the very One Who had been crucified. That this was the effect of His words and His action is proved by the statement of John, " The disciples therefore were glad when they saw the Lord."

He then repeated the salutation, this time following it by the declaration that He was about to send them forth on His work. The first " Peace unto you " was His answer to their fear, and the argument was Himself, wounded and yet living. The second " Peace unto you " was preparation for their service, and the argument was His authority to send, demonstrated by His victory over death.

In connection with the second salutation He breathed on them symbolically, and prophetically, saying as He did so, " Receive ye the Holy Spirit." It is evident that they did not then receive the Spirit, because the same evening, as Luke records, He charged them to wait until they were clothed with power from on high. The remarkable, sacred, and solemn ministry of dealing with sin, either by way of remission or retention, did not commence until after the Pentecostal effusion, upon which it was entirely dependent.

In all the life and service of the days that followed, that double salutation of the risen Lord must have been of unspeakable value, reminding them, in the presence of fear, of the fact that He was alive in victory over death; and in the activity of service, that they acted under His authority, and in the power of His Spirit.

ii. THOMAS

Very beautiful was the Lord's dealing with Thomas, who having been absent from that first evening assembly, declined to believe that the Lord was risen, unless he received the same demonstration which had been granted to the rest.

John here recorded another appearance of the Master eight days later, in order that His method with Thomas might be revealed. Mary, too easily satisfied with earthly relationship, He did not permit to touch Him. Thomas, unable to believe

in the continuity of lost relationship, He
invited to touch Him and handle Him,
that his faith might be strengthened.
The wisdom and perfection of the Master's
method as manifested in the glory of
the light which flooded the spirit of the
honest sceptic, is revealed in the magnificence of his confession, " My Lord and
My God."

iii. Unrecorded Signs

John closed this section of his record
by words which give us the key not only
to the post-resurrection stories, but to the
method of the whole book. He did not
write all the signs which Jesus wrought,
but enough to give light which would lead
to belief resulting in possession of life.

III. ABIDING LOVE

i. Breakfast

After a dark and fruitless night of
labour, how glorious was the morning
light! The great beauty of this story lies

in its revelation of the interest of the risen Word in the commonplace affairs of His people. He was interested in their fishing, and knew how to direct them even in that, so that it should be successful. He was interested in their physical conditions, and Himself built a fire, and prepared a breakfast, that they might be warmed and fed after the wearisome experiences of the night of fruitless toil.

This interest is all the more remarkable when we remember that the action of the disciples in going fishing was in all probability that of restless unbelief. He had distinctly called them long ago from such avocation, and had indicated their work when He had told them that He would make them fishers of men. It is very evident that during these strange and wonderful days they were perplexed beyond measure, and this action of going fishing on the proposition of Peter was a sign of their uncertainty of mind. Perhaps they did not go back, with any intention of taking up again the abandoned calling, but only in order to ease the strain of restlessness through which they were passing. Be that as it may, this at least is certain, that there was no rebuke in our Lord's attitude towards them, although it is not without significance that the toilings of the night were fruitless.

ii. LOVE TRIUMPHANT

In all the story of the Master's dealings with His disciples, there is nothing more exquisite than this account of the patience and power of His method with Peter. Great was the purpose of the Lord for this man when He first called him, and although in the terrible stress of the days when it seemed to him that the mission of Jesus was failing, his courage had failed, that first purpose of the Master could not be ultimately defeated. Nevertheless the failure had been of such a nature that his restoration to the place of fellowship and service needed to be as definite, clear, and public, as had been the degradation.

Peter had denied his Lord by the side of a fire built by His foes. He must now confess Him by the side of a fire built by Himself. Thrice was the denial repeated, and thrice must the confession be made. The contrasts are as striking as are the similarities. The denial was in the darkness of the night, the confession in the dawning glow of the morning. The denial was the answer of cowardice to the sarcasm of hatred; the confession was the answer of courage to the strength of Love. The confession moreover, was of such a nature as to go far beyond the denial. He had denied knowledge of Christ. He now confessed love to Christ.

After each confession He was commissioned for special service; the Lord thus revealing to him, and to His people for ever, His willingness to repose perfect confidence in those who sincerely love Him.

A careful study of the story reveals at once the tender grace of the Lord and the new humility and consequent strength of Peter. The word for love which Christ used in the first two inquiries was the highest possible word, suggesting love as more than emotion, being rather devotion based upon clear intellectual apprehension. To this, the high word, Peter, with fine humility, never dared to aspire, using rather in his affirmation in each case the tender, emotional word of human friendship. In the last challenge Jesus took Peter's own word. It was this fact that grieved Peter, and yet is it not proof beyond all others of the sensitive sympathy and patience of the Master? It is interesting to remember that when in after years this man came to write his letters, he used the word which Jesus first used.

In the process of restoration the final word of Jesus was one by which he led Peter back to the Cross which he had hunned at Cæsarea Philippi, and laid upon him the command, "Follow Me."

The beauty of the whole story is enhanced by the glimpse John gives of Peter beyond the restoration, as he attempted to make arrangements for John in the days to come; and of Jesus as He gently rebuked him, and indicated His own authority over all His disciples.

iii. UNRECORDED DEEDS

Full of interest are the last words of John, in which he affirmed that he had written little, in the words, " There are also many other things which Jesus did, the which, if they should be written every one, I suppose that even the world itself would not contain the books which should be written."

Thus he closed as he began. His first statement was concerning the Eternal Word; his last that words can never express all the facts, even of His tabernacling in the flesh.

Thus as at the beginning of the Gospel we stood in wonder in the presence of the bewildering eternities, at the close we stand in amazement in view of the infinitudes which have yet been revealed in a Person upon Whom we may look, to Whom we may listen, Whom indeed we may handle, Who yet for ever defies any to say all that is to be said concerning Him.